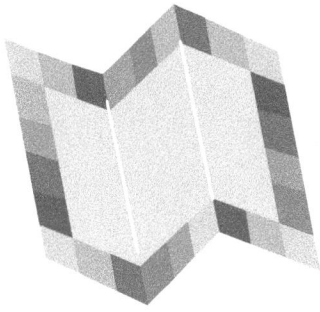

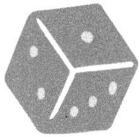

THE *GAME* THERAPY TOOLBOX

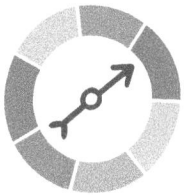

114 Innovative Activities to Help Kids Address Anxiety, Trauma, Grief, Attachment, Self-Regulation, Social Skills, Family Relationships, and More

Liana Lowenstein, MSW, RSW, CPT-S

THE GAME THERAPY TOOLBOX
Copyright © 2025 by Liana Lowenstein

Published by
PESI Publishing, Inc.
3839 White Ave
Eau Claire, WI 54703

Cover and interior design by Emily Dyer
Editing by Kate Sample

ISBN 9781683738398 (print)
ISBN 9781683738404 (ePUB)
ISBN 9781683738411 (ePDF)

PESI Publishing
pesipublishing.com

Table of Contents

Activities at a Glance

Family Interaction			
Activity	**Ages**	**Modality**	**Page**
Cooperation and Compliments	6–12	Family	240
Family Avatar Quest	8+	Family	243
Family Communication with Miniature Figurines	8+	Family	245
Family Tree in Minecraft	7+	Family	247
Nature's Treasures Tic-Tac-Toe	6+	Family	249
Paparazzi	8+	Family	251
Photographs and Memories	7+	Family	253
Teen Talk	12+	Family	256
Toss the Ball	8+	Family	259
Totem of Appreciation	8+	Family	261
Upside-Down Tower of Positives	8+	Family	262
What Would They Say?	8+	Family	263
Termination			
Activity	**Ages**	**Modality**	**Page**
Balloon Bash	6–10	Individual	268
The Family Bowl	8+	Family	271
Last Session Family Card Game	7+	Family	273
Minute to Win It	7–14	Individual	276
Nature Shapes Scavenger Hunt	5+	Group, Family	278
Therapy Treasure Hunt	7–10	Individual	280

Introduction

Mozart was just five years old when he composed his first piece of music. Louis Braille invented his famous tactile writing system at fifteen. And me? I was eight when I created my very first game . . . for my pet hamster! I built a miniature obstacle course from cardboard, with tunnels, ramps, and tiny treat-filled puzzles for my hamster to navigate. While my furry friend didn't seem all that impressed, watching him explore was endlessly entertaining and sparked my love for creating games.

The pivotal moment of my game-making was in my early teen years, when I was a tutor for elementary school kids. I remember a seven-year-old girl who looked sullen and not at all interested in the math we were working on. I was struggling to get her to look at me, let alone her work. So, instead of repeating myself teaching her in a traditional way, I whipped up a simple subtraction game to make it fun. And guess what? Her face lit up, she was more excited to learn, and she gained confidence in her ability to do math that day! I was on to something.

Fifty years and thousands of therapy clients later, games are still a foundational element in how I work therapeutically with kids and families in my office.

I love seeing the magic that happens when playful techniques turn therapy into something meaningful, engaging, and empowering—and I want to teach you how to bring that magic to your own practice.

What Is Game Therapy?

Simply put, game therapy is using games and playfulness to achieve therapeutic outcomes.

It's like a secret weapon therapists can use to help kids and families tackle tough emotional and behavioral challenges. A simple board or card game can open a door to a world where kids feel safe to express themselves and families can learn to communicate, heal, and grow stronger together. In other words, games aren't just fun—they're powerful therapeutic tools (Stone & Schaefer, 2020). Here's why:

- **Building trust:** Games help create a positive rapport between therapists and clients by providing a relaxed and enjoyable environment where barriers can come down naturally. Through shared play, trust develops as the child sees the therapist as a safe and approachable figure.

- **Emotional expression:** Games provide a creative outlet for kids to share feelings they might not be able to verbalize. By engaging in activities like role-playing or storytelling, children can project their emotions onto the game, making it easier to explore and discuss them.

- **Safe space:** Games create a nonthreatening way to approach difficult topics like anxiety or trauma. The structured yet playful environment of a game can reduce stress and defensiveness, allowing clients to process emotions in manageable steps.

- **Social skills:** Games naturally teach prosocial behaviors like cooperation, turn-taking, and conflict resolution by requiring players to follow rules, work together, and navigate disagreements. Practicing these skills in a fun and low-pressure context builds confidence for real-world interactions.

- **Brain boost:** The strategic and problem-solving elements of games stimulate cognitive growth, improving attention, creativity, and critical thinking. Games that involve quick decision-making or planning ahead challenge the brain to develop new connections and skills.

- **Family bonding and communication:** Games strengthen family bonds by encouraging shared experiences that are enjoyable and meaningful. When families play together, they practice communication skills like active listening, expressing themselves clearly, and resolving conflicts in a safe environment. Games also provide opportunities for each family member to feel heard and valued, especially in cooperative or team-based activities where everyone has a role to play. Through the shared joy of play, families build trust, enhance understanding, and create positive memories that improve their overall connection.

What's in This Book

The Game Therapy Toolbox is a collection of therapeutic games derived from decades of not only my clinical experience but that of my amazing colleagues in the play therapy field. In these pages you will find over 100 games designed to help build therapeutic rapport, teach important skills, overcome therapeutic roadblocks, and improve family relationships.

You'll find a variety of games for different ages and clinical issues. Some are based on traditional games you likely already have in your office, while others are unique creations. The interventions use inexpensive, easy-to-find materials and can be easily implemented in a variety of settings, like a therapy office, schools, and the client's home.

The chapters in this book focus on different themes, including common presenting problems, stages of treatment, and other key aspects of therapy with children and families:

1. Rapport building

2. Feelings expression

3. Focus and self-regulation

4. Social skills

5. Anxiety and fears

6. Trauma and stress

7. Self-esteem

8. Family interaction

9. Termination

Each chapter offers a variety of game therapy interventions so you can select those most appropriate to your client's age, interests, and needs.

How to Use This Book

This book is a treasure trove for mental health professionals looking to spice up their sessions with therapeutic games. Remember to use these games as part of a broader clinical strategy, based on thorough assessments and case planning. It is essential to use therapeutic games in a clinically and theoretically sound manner and pay special attention to the process underlying each technique.

Choosing the Game

Choosing the right game is key! You'll want to consider the client's "age and stage"; that is, determine which games are developmentally appropriate in content, difficulty, and accessibility. And of course, choose a game that interests the child. You'll also want to consider the client's therapeutic goals. Choose a game that aligns with what you're working on, whether it's social skills, anxiety, distress tolerance, or family dynamics, to name a few. The activities in this book are organized by theme and labeled with the recommended ages and modalities (individual, group, and/or family) to assist you in the selection process.

Adaptation and Creativity

When incorporating games into sessions, be playful to promote child engagement. Adapt the games as needed to fit the specific context and therapeutic goals. Add your own creative ideas and encourage the child to do the same. This makes therapy more engaging and empowering.

It is also important to balance the need to maintain the flow and engagement of the game while addressing therapeutic goals. For instance, if a client is struggling with negative self-talk, you might introduce a game character who models positive self-talk, thereby providing the client with a relatable example.

Points of Departure

As clients engage in the game, they often begin to talk about issues that are important to them. A key concept in game play therapy is "points of departure," in which players "leave" the game to discuss issues expressed during the game (Schaefer & Reid, 2001). As an example, consider a ten-year-old child who talks about feeling sad about being bullied. While playing a cooperative board game, the child might mention how a character in the game reminds them of a bully at school. This moment serves as a point of departure, where the game is paused to explore the child's feelings and experiences related to bullying. Open-ended questions can enhance the brief discussion, such as, "How did that make you feel?" or "Tell me more about the bullying that you have experienced." By addressing the child's emotions in the context of the game, the child has an opportunity to express and process their feelings. After briefly discussing the issue, players return to playing the game.

Therapeutic Responses

It is important to employ a range of clinical skills to facilitate effective game therapy. Active listening is paramount, ensuring that the client feels heard and validated. Empathy helps in building a trusting relationship, making the client more comfortable in expressing their feelings. Reflective questioning can guide the client to gain insights into their own experiences and emotions. For example, you might say, "It sounds like you felt very alone when that happened. Is that right?" This not only validates the client's feelings but also encourages deeper self-reflection.

During gameplay, there are many opportunities to respond or to make statements that are inherent to your work and therapeutic for the client. Here are some examples, using the game of pick-up sticks:

- **Validate:** "You feel frustrated when you move a stick."

- **Empathize:** "This is a difficult turn for you because the sticks are so close together."

- **Reflect feelings:** "You feel proud of yourself for getting that stick."

- **Model open expression:** "I feel jealous that you're winning!"

- **Model skill:** "I'm going to go slow and really concentrate."

- **Model following the rules:** "I was going to pretend that the other stick didn't move, but I'm going to play by the rules so it's fair for both of us."

- **Affirm perseverance:** "That was a hard move, but you tried anyway!"

- **Encourage flexible thinking:** "You were planning on trying for this stick but then I got it, so now you have to try for a different one."

- **Compliment:** "Great job waiting patiently for your turn!"

- **Cheerlead:** "Go, Johnny!"

- **Demonstrate playfulness:** "Woohoo!"

By following this advice and your own clinical judgment, you can bring the therapeutic power—and fun!—of game therapy to your sessions. So, flip through this book, choose games that seem like the right fit for your clients, and see the magic unfold!

References

Schaefer, C. E., & Reid, S. E. (2001). *Game play: Therapeutic use of childhood games* (2nd ed.). Wiley.

Stone, J., & Schaefer, C. E. (Eds.). (2020). *Game play: Therapeutic use of games with children and adolescents* (3rd ed.). Wiley.

CHAPTER 1

Building Therapeutic Rapport

Many children are anxious about the therapeutic process. The fun aspect of gameplay can engage children in therapy and can help them develop a sense of safety. When the therapist and client are jointly engaged in a game, it provides an ideal opportunity to strengthen the therapeutic relationship. Additionally, games create a nonthreatening environment where children feel more comfortable expressing themselves.

Through structured play, children are able to share their thoughts, worries, and emotions more naturally, fostering trust. The shared experience of playing also allows the therapist to observe social cues, emotional reactions, and relational patterns in a less formal setting. These insights can be critical in building a deeper understanding of the child, which in turn strengthens therapeutic outcomes.

This chapter offers a number of games that can facilitate rapport building. While these games provide useful strategies to engage children, remember that it is the therapist's use of self that is the most powerful engagement tool in the therapy room. The therapist's warmth, consistency, and unconditional acceptance of the child are key ingredients to put the child at ease and help develop a therapeutic alliance.

21: A RAPPORT-BUILDING GAME

Introduction

This game is designed to create a safe and engaging environment for therapeutic interactions, allowing participants to build rapport and share personal information in a structured yet enjoyable manner. By combining the familiar rules of the card game "21" with guided questions, it helps facilitate open communication and mutual understanding between players.

Goals

- Establish a safe and open therapeutic environment
- Gather information about the client

Materials

- *Get to Know You Questions* list (provided on page 284)
- Standard 52-card deck

Instructions

1. Explain the rules of the game to the client:
   - The object of "21" is to have the sum of your cards be equal to or as close to 21 as possible without going over—and to have a higher sum than the other player.
   - Number cards are represented by their respective face value. Jacks, kings, and queens are each worth 10. Aces can be either 1 or 11 (the player who holds the ace gets to choose the value of the card).

2. After shuffling the deck, deal the client and yourself one card each, face up, and then a second card each, face down. (Or you can make the game more transparent by dealing all four cards face up.) Each player privately looks at their face-down card and adds up their two cards' total value in their mind.

3. The client goes first. They can decide to "stay"—that is, keep the hand they were dealt and not receive additional cards—if they are satisfied with their total as-is, or they can request another card from the dealer (you) by saying "hit me" to try to get their total closer to 21. They may hit any number of times until they are satisfied with their total or until they go over 21 and "bust." Deal any new cards face up.

4. Take your own turn, with the same options of staying or hitting until you either are satisfied with your total or go bust.

5. Each player reveals their hidden card and therefore the total value of their cards. The player whose total is closest to 21 without going over wins. The winner of each round gets to choose a "getting to know you" question to ask the other player. (See the list provided.) Play several rounds of the game.

CANDY LAND: RAPPORT-BUILDING VERSION*

AGES: 4–8   **MODALITY:** INDIVIDUAL, GROUP, FAMILY

Introduction

This activity uses the classic Candy Land game to help build therapeutic rapport. As players move around the board, they answer questions that help them become better acquainted. This activity is designed to create a positive environment where clients feel comfortable and open to talking.

Goals

- Begin to establish a positive and open therapeutic environment
- Gather information about the client

Materials

- Candy Land board game
- *Get to Know You Questions* list (provided on page 284)

Advance Preparation

- Before the session, if needed, prepare a list of questions tailored to the needs of the client(s). Otherwise, use the list provided.

Instructions

1. Each player chooses a pawn to represent themselves and places it on the starting square.

2. Players take turns picking a card from the deck. If the color on the card is different from their pawn's square or if they pick a picture card, they must answer a "get to know you" question before moving to the appropriate square on the game board. If the card's color matches their pawn's square, they get to move immediately to that color and get an extra turn without answering a question.

3. You can adjust the frequency of the questions by changing the rules; for example, you could say that players only need to answer a question when they land on a square that is the same color as their pawn.

4. Afterward, ask process questions such as:
   - Say something you learned about someone from this game.
   - What was your favorite question?
   - Was there a question that was hard for you to answer? Why?

---

*   Intervention by Gary G. F. Yorke, PhD

FIRST SESSION FAMILY CARD GAME*

AGES: 7+   **MODALITY:** FAMILY

Introduction

This game is designed to help family members engage in a fun and interactive way during their initial therapy session. It aims to assess family dynamics, promote open communication, and highlight both the positive aspects of family life and areas in need of change. Through game-based interactions, the family is encouraged to share, reflect, and explore their relationships with the support of a therapist.

Goals

- Join with the family
- Assess family relationships and dynamics
- Identify positive aspects of family life and pinpoint areas for change

Materials

- *First Family Session Card Game* question cards (provided)
- Cardstock
- Scissors
- Standard 52-card deck
- Cookies or other rewards

Advance Preparation

- Photocopy the question cards provided onto cardstock and cut them into cards or copy the questions onto index cards.

Instructions

1. Introduce the activity by stating, "We are going to play a game that will help me get to know your family." The rules are explained as follows: "Take turns picking the top card from the deck of playing cards. If you get a card with an even number, pick a question card and answer the question. If you get a card with an odd number, pick a question card and ask someone in your family to answer the question. If you do not feel you can answer the question, you can ask your family for help. If you pick an ace, ask someone in your family for a hug, fist bump, or high five. If you pick a jack, do 10 jumping jacks. If you pick a queen or king, you get a cookie. At the end of the game, everyone who played gets a cookie."

---

* Adapted from "First Session Family Card Game," by L. Lowenstein, in L. Lowenstein (Ed.), *Creative Family Therapy Techniques: Play, Art, and Expressive Activities to Engage Children in Family Sessions* (2010), Champion Press.

2. Encourage active discussion among the family during the game. You may wish to stop the game periodically to expand on feelings or issues disclosed by the family members, even jotting down notes and saying, "I want to remember these important things about your family."

3. After the game, ask process questions such as:

   - What new information did you learn about your family?
   - What was the most interesting or surprising response?
   - How difficult or easy was it to answer the questions?

Fill in the blank: Our family is here today because...

Fill in the blank: A good therapist is someone who...

What do you want to know about your therapist?

Define family therapy. (You can ask the therapist to help.)

What sorts of problems usually bring a family to therapy? (You can ask the therapist to help.)

What would need to happen in the session today to make you feel like it was worthwhile coming?

Say one word that best describes how you feel about being here today.

Who decided you should seek help at this time?

What is a question or worry you have about family therapy?

Explain what you've done before to try to solve the main problem that brought you here today.

Switch seats with the person who you think is the most affected by the problem.

Tell about a time when things at home were better.

?	?	?
Who, outside of your family, has helped you in the past?	What would your parent or sibling say needs to change in your family?	What do you think needs to change in your family?
Describe what it would be like in your family if the problems were gone.	True or false: When families see a therapist they often feel nervous, embarrassed, and overwhelmed.	Of the goals that have been identified today, which is the most important to you?
True or false: Everyone in our family plays a part in making it better.	Switch seats with the person you think is most willing to change in your family.	What is the most important thing for the therapist to know about your family?
True or false: Only crazy people go to therapy.	Switch seats with the person who is the easiest to talk to about problems and worries.	How will you feel if you or your family gets the help you need?

GETTING TO KNOW EACH OTHER DICE GAME*

AGES: 7+   **MODALITY:** INDIVIDUAL

Introduction

This game is designed to facilitate a positive and open therapeutic environment, encouraging participants to share personal information in an engaging and interactive way using dice. It helps build rapport and promotes better understanding and connection.

Goals

- Establish a positive and open therapeutic environment
- Gather information about the client

Materials

- *Get to Know You Questions* (provided on page 284)
- Two dice

Instructions

1. Explain to the client that this game will help you get to know each other.

2. Share the directions for the game: "To play, we will take turns rolling the dice. If we roll an even number, we will choose any question from the list and answer it about ourselves. If we roll an odd number, we will choose any question from the list for the other person to answer. We will play until we have each had five turns."

---

* Adapted from *Creative Interventions for Bereaved Children* (2nd ed.), by L. Lowenstein (2024), Champion Press.

HIDE AND FIND*

AGES: 4–8   **MODALITY:** INDIVIDUAL

Introduction

This intervention addresses therapy goals for children who have challenges in establishing relationships and meaningful connection with others. The game provides several opportunities for the client to practice relationship and connection.

Goals

- Establish a positive therapeutic rapport
- Increase playful interaction between child and therapist (or child and caregiver)

Materials

- Index cards
- Marker or colored pencil

Advance Preparation

- Write seven connection activities on index cards and hide the index cards around the room. These connection activities should be short and simple (e.g., shake hands, say hello with your eyes, give each other a fist bump, give a double high five, give each other a pat on the back, do a salute, or create a secret handshake).

Instructions

1. Explain: "This game is called 'Hide and Find.' I have hidden seven index cards around the room for you to find. Once you find a card, we must do the activity written on the card."

2. The game ends once all the cards have been found and all the activities have been completed.

---

*   Intervention by Robert Jason Grant, EdD, LPC, RPT-S™. Adapted with permission from *Play Interventions for Neurodivergent Children and Adolescents: Promoting Growth, Empowerment, and Affirming Practices*, by R. J. Grant (2024), Routledge.

NATURE BINGO*

Introduction

This game offers an engaging way for participants to explore the outdoors while building a positive therapeutic rapport. It combines creativity and interaction with nature, encouraging participants to be present in the moment and enjoy their surroundings while working toward completing their bingo cards.

Goals

- Begin to establish a positive therapeutic rapport
- Build a sense of accomplishment

Materials

- Poster board
- Markers
- Images of items found in nature
- Scissors
- Glue or tape
- Bag
- Stickers

Advance Preparation

- Print out, cut out from magazines, or draw images of nature items (e.g., flowers, insects, leaves, birds) that can be found in your area, making all the images roughly the same size. Prepare at least 15 images per player. Place the images in the bag. Next, create blank bingo cards (one per player) out of poster board. Each card should be a 3×3 grid that will fit nine of the nature images.

Instructions

1. Provide each player with a blank bingo card. Let them know this game is about having fun in nature and working together.

2. Instruct each player to create their bingo card by choosing nine images from the bag and adhering them to each of the spaces on their card using glue or tape.

3. Give each player nine stickers. Explain: "To play this game, we will go outside to see if we can find each of the items on our board out in the nature around us. Each time you find a nature item that is on your card, put a sticker on that image. When you have found all nine items on your bingo card, you will yell 'Bingo!' as loudly as you want! This means you are the winner!"

---

* Intervention by Jamie Lynn Langley, LCSW, RPT-S™

4. Take the players outside and complete the game, offering assistance as needed.

5. Follow up with process questions such as:

  - How did it feel to explore nature in this way?

  - What was your favorite item you found on your bingo card?

  - How does spending time outside change how you feel?

  - What can you do next time to look for different things in nature?

PARTNER PERFECTION*

AGES: 8+   **MODALITY:** INDIVIDUAL

Introduction

This activity uses the game Perfection as a therapeutic tool to establish rapport with the client and create a positive, supportive environment. It helps children understand the benefits of working together with their therapist to accomplish goals, easing their anxiety about therapy and setting the tone for collaboration.

Goals

- Establish a positive therapeutic environment
- Verbally articulate the benefits of therapeutic support

Materials

- Perfection game by Hasbro

Instructions

1. Explain how to play the game as usual: The timer is set and started, the board is pushed down, and the object is to place as many pieces in the correct slot as they can before the timer goes off. Warn the client ahead of time about what happens when the game's timer goes off (it buzzes loudly and board pops up, causing the pieces to scatter), as this can be scary for children, especially if they have not played this game before.

2. Invite the client to play the game. Reflect the client's process and cheer for them as they attempt to beat the clock. Normalize that most people are not able to get all the pieces in the correct slot before the timer goes off, especially on the first try.

3. Regardless of whether they do complete it on their first try, introduce the idea of working on it together: "I wonder it would go if we did it together, as a team."

4. After playing the game together, reflect on how it was easier to get all (or more) pieces into the slots before the timer went off. Connect their reflection with the therapy process by saying something like, "Therapy can be scary, confusing, or sometimes hard without support, but we are going to work together to accomplish your goals just like we did in the game."

5. Ask process questions such as:
   - How did you feel when you were trying to get the pieces in before the timer went off?
   - What was different when we worked together as a team?
   - Describe a time when something was hard to do alone, but easier with help.
   - How does this game remind you of things we can work on together in therapy?

---

* Intervention by Kelly Pullen, MA, LPC-S, RPT™

ROCK, PAPER, SCISSORS*

Introduction

Introducing a familiar game like "rock, paper, scissors" into a therapeutic setting provides a comfortable and engaging way for children to open up and share personal information. Most children know the game, which allows them to easily participate and enjoy the activity. This facilitates a positive rapport and open conversation.

Goals

- Begin to establish a positive and open therapeutic environment
- Gather information about the client

Materials

- *Get to Know You Questions* (provided on page 284)
- Scissors
- Small gift bag or box

Advance Preparation

- Cut out the questions and place them in the gift bag or box.

Instructions

1. Play rock, paper, scissors the standard way.

2. The winner of each round gets to ask the other player a "get to know you" question from the bag or make up their own question to ask. If it's a tie, play until someone wins.

---

* Intervention by Angela Cavett, PhD

THREE FOAM DICE*

AGES: 7–12   **MODALITY:** INDIVIDUAL

Introduction

This playful intervention focuses on positive interactions with another person and deepening relationship development. Three large foam dice are used in a game format to allow for the therapist and child to engage in a variety of ways.

Goals

- Establish a positive and open therapeutic environment
- Gather information about the client

Materials

- Three large foam dice
- Permanent markers

Advance Preparation

- Prepare the foam dice by writing the following prompts on them. Make sure you do not obscure the dots as you do so. Consider the individual child you are working with—their age, presenting concern, accommodations, and any disability needs they may have—when formulating your prompts.
  - On each side of the first die, write a question to ask other people (you can use the *Get to Know You Questions* on page 284 or create your own).
  - On each side of the second die, write something to share about yourself (e.g., favorite movie, hobbies, childhood memories).
  - On each side of the third die, write an activity to do together (e.g., throw a ball back and forth, thumb wrestle, give each other a high five).

Instructions

1. Explain to the client that you're going to play a dice game to get to know each other better.

2. Take turns rolling all three dice at once. Whatever is displayed on the upside of each die is what the client and therapist will do, and the number on the die signifies the number of times they will do it. For example, if the upside of the die says, "What is your favorite color?" and has three dots on it, the person being asked shares their three favorite colors.

3. Continue to play until you have implemented everything written on the dice or until you think it is appropriate to end the game.

---

* Intervention by Robert Jason Grant, EdD, LPC, RPT-S™. Adapted with permission from *Play Interventions for Neurodivergent Children and Adolescents: Promoting Growth, Empowerment, and Affirming Practices,* by R. J. Grant (2024), Routledge.

TIKTOK TALK

Introduction

Using social media platforms offers a unique opportunity to engage clients in therapeutic activities, allowing entry into their world and facilitating meaningful conversations. This game uses the popular app TikTok to create a safe environment where clients can express themselves, share their interests, and foster self-esteem through guided discussions and interactive prompts.

Goals

- Establish a safe and open therapeutic environment
- Gather information about the client

Materials

- Computer, tablet, or phone with internet access and the TikTok app installed
- One die (online or the game piece)

Note: Be mindful of the client's comfort level with sharing personal content from their TikTok account.

Instructions

1. Have the client roll the die. The number they get represents the question to be asked from the following list:

   - 1 = Show me a TikTok video that was created by someone else that you really like. Why do you like it?
   - 2 = Show me a video you created that you really like. What inspired you to make it?
   - 3 = Show me a video that is funny. Why do you think it's funny?
   - 4 = Show me a video that inspires you. How does it inspire you?
   - 5 = Show me a video that taught you something. What did you learn?
   - 6 = Show me a video of your choice. Why did you choose this one?

2. Invite the client to share the corresponding TikTok video with you and answer the question provided. Ask follow-up questions to gain deeper insights into the client's thoughts, feelings, and personality. Tailor the follow-up questions and discussions to suit the individual needs and therapeutic goals of each client.

3. Have the client continue rolling the die until all six questions are answered. In a group setting, participants can take turns doing this.

WHAT'S IN THE BAG?: 20 QUESTIONS

Introduction

This is a pre-session activity that is conducted virtually ahead of the client's first session with you. It is geared toward children who are reluctant to attend therapy or who are highly anxious about their initial session to help build rapport and positive feelings about attending therapy with you. It is designed to get kids excited about their first session and to put them at ease once they are there, creating a fun and engaging therapeutic environment right from the start.

Goals

- Increase the child's motivation to attend therapy
- Put the child at ease
- Establish a positive therapeutic environment

Materials: None

Instructions

1. Schedule a brief virtual "meet and greet" session with the child and their caregiver several days prior to the scheduled in-person session.

2. Once online with the client, begin this virtual session with casual chitchat. Then let the child know you would like them to bring an item from home to their first session with you. They should not tell you what it is, and they should hide it in a bag or box. When the client arrives for their first in-person session, you will play "20 questions" to guess what the client brought. The idea is to create something to look forward to at your first session together and for you to show your playful side so that their upcoming visit feels less daunting.

3. When the child arrives for their in-person session, express excitement about seeing them, praise them for remembering to bring the item, and begin the game of 20 questions. If you correctly guess what's in the bag, give an enthusiastic "Woohoo!" If you don't guess what's in the bag, comment on how clever the child was to choose an item that was so difficult to guess. Keep in mind that the aim of the session is on therapeutic engagement, so guessing what's in the bag is less important than the process of rapport building. If needed, make plans with the child to do it again at your next session together.

YES/NO JUMPING GAME

AGES: 4–8   **MODALITY:** INDIVIDUAL

Introduction

Building rapport with children is crucial in therapy, as it creates a safe and open environment for them to express themselves. Engaging the child in a physically active game like this one will help you gather valuable information about their interests and strengths while channeling their anxious energy into a positive outlet.

Goals

- Establish a safe and open therapeutic environment
- Gather information about the client

Materials

- *Yes/No Jumping Game Prompts* list (provided)
- Two large pieces of paper
- Thick marker

Instructions

1. Write *YES* on one large piece of paper and *NO* on the other. Place the two papers on the floor at least four feet apart.

2. Explain that you will ask the client questions to get to know them, what they like, and so on. Their way of answering will be to jump on the piece of paper with their answer on it. Choose questions to ask from the *Yes/No Jumping Game Prompts* list and note the client's responses.

3. Consider taking turns asking or jumping with the client, if appropriate, or have the client come up with their own yes/no questions for you.

YES/NO JUMPING GAME PROMPTS

- I like to watch TV.

- I love ice cream.

- I like to draw and do crafts.

- I play video games very well.

- I have a sister.

- I'm athletic and enjoy playing sports.

- I am kind to people.

- I like to play outside.

- I am 100 years old.

- I am an amazing builder and I like to create stuff with LEGO.

- I enjoy music (listening to music, singing, playing an instrument).

- I have a wonderful imagination.

- I have purple hair.

- I can dance really well.

- I'm great with animals.

- I have good ideas that I like to share in school.

- I like to go swimming.

- I like scary things like movies, shows, or haunted houses.

- Summer is my favorite season.

- I have been on an airplane before.

LEVEL UP YOUR THERAPY: GAME-BASED REASSESSMENT*

AGES: 12+   **MODALITY:** INDIVIDUAL, FAMILY

Introduction

This engaging activity incorporates games as well as the client's input into the process of reviewing and updating their treatment plan. This fun and interactive approach not only makes therapy more enjoyable but also ensures that the client has a voice in shaping their path to progress.

Goals

- Increase the client's level of engagement and motivation in therapy
- Obtain input from the client on the treatment plan

Materials

- Variety of board and card games (e.g., UNO, Sorry!)

Instructions

1. Explain, "For every client, I write a treatment plan that describes why you have come to me for help, the priority goals we are focusing on, and how we are going to work toward achieving those goals. Sometimes it is best that we have a meeting about how things are going so that we can update the treatment plan. You are the expert on you, and for that reason I'd like the plan to include your thoughts and ideas. You might have some ideas on things that we could be doing in here that are way more helpful and fun than my ideas!"

2. Then explain that you would like to update the treatment plan in the least boring way possible by playing a game. Say, "In between rounds of the game, I can ask you things that I'd like your thoughts on, such as something that went just a tiny bit better at school this year or something that's been really giving you a hard time with friends lately. I might also throw in some easier questions, like your favorite type of ice cream, because those things are important too!"

3. Be creative and collaborate with the client to modify this intervention in a way that will be engaging and helpful. For example, one of my favorite ways to do this is with UNO and a set of "would you rather" cards. Each time the client wins a game, they get to draw a "would you rather" question for me to answer, and each time I win, I get to ask them a reassessment question. You could also use the game Sorry! and have the client answer a question every time they get out of start or in home. The options are endless!

4. It is important to tailor questions to the client's developmental level. For example, for younger clients, keep the questions short and simple while moving the game along at a brisk pace. For older clients, ask a follow-up question before moving on to the next round of the game.

---

* Intervention by Katy Delagardelle, LISW

It is helpful to assure the client that there are no wrong answers. Examples of reassessment questions include:

- What has been one of your favorite moments throughout therapy so far?
- Describe a proud moment that shows your progress in therapy.
- If therapy was a game, what level do you think you're on right now, and what would it take to reach the next level?
- What is slowing you down from making even more progress than you already have?
- If you could change one thing about the way we do therapy, what would it be?
- What would need to happen in therapy for you to feel like it was more helpful?
- What is a change you would like to make that would improve your life, and how can therapy help you make this change?
- What is something about your life that is bothering or upsetting you, that you have control over?
- What goal do you want to work on next with me, and what are your ideas for creative activities (like art or games) that could help you achieve this goal?
- What advice do you have for me on how I can be the best therapist possible for you?
- How will you know when it's time to end therapy and plan a graduation session?

CHAPTER 2

Expression of Feelings

Many children, particularly those who have experienced trauma, lack the emotional, cognitive, and verbal abilities to identify and communicate their feelings directly and in a healthy manner. Children may also suppress their feelings or restrict their feelings vocabulary to basic emotions like happy, sad, and mad. In such cases, children need both permission to express themselves openly and the skills to enhance their feelings vocabulary so they can identify and articulate a broader range of emotional states.

When children are limited in their ability to talk about their feelings, it can help to combine discussion with engaging therapeutic games. The games in this chapter provide a structured yet playful environment, helping children verbalize and express their feelings with reduced levels of anxiety. Through interactive play, children are often more willing to share vulnerable emotions that they may otherwise avoid.

Games encourage emotional regulation and allow children to explore different emotions in a safe space. This chapter will introduce various types of games that target emotional literacy, offering creative ways to assist children in processing their emotions. These interventions can help clients build confidence in expressing their inner world, leading to improved emotional well-being and self-awareness.

ACT AS IF*

Introduction

One of the best ways to learn something is by doing. In Adlerian Play Therapy, we engage in experiential learning by "acting as if." This means stepping into another person's shoes to see with their eyes, hear with their ears, and feel with their heart. This approach helps clients explore different perspectives and develop deeper understanding and empathy in a safe and playful environment. Through role-playing various characters, emotions, and situations, clients can experiment with new ways of thinking and behaving, which can lead to meaningful personal growth. This game is an engaging way for clients to develop social and emotional skills.

Goals

- Express a range of emotions
- Learn and practice empathy
- Foster creativity and problem-solving abilities

Materials

- *"Act As If" Characters, Feelings, and Situations* list (provided)
- One d20 die (die with numbers 1–20)
- Paper and a writing utensil

Instructions

1. Each player rolls the die three times, taking note of which numbers are rolled.

2. Using the *"Act As If" Characters, Feelings, and Situations* list, match the first number rolled with the corresponding character, the second with the feeling, and the third with the situation.

3. The player who rolled will then act as if they are that character, with that feeling, in that situation. If the player cannot find a creative way to act out the scenario, they can choose one die to re-roll. If the player is not familiar with the character, you can describe them and substitute a similar character (e.g., another superhero) if needed.

4. Ask process questions such as:
   - How did it feel to be the one acting?
   - How did it feel to be the one observing?
   - Were there any combinations that stood out to you? Why?
   - If you could choose one character to "act as if" in certain situations, who might you choose and in what situation would you want to choose them for? Why?
   - Does this activity remind you of real life? Why or why not?

---

* Intervention by Erika Walker, LSCSW, LCSW, LICSW, RPT-S™

"ACT AS IF" CHARACTERS, FEELINGS, AND SITUATIONS

Characters	Feelings	Situations
1. Bluey	1. Calm	1. Received a gift
2. Glinda	2. Energized	2. Got in trouble
3. The Joker	3. Frustrated	3. Was bullied
4. Spider-Man	4. Brave	4. Argued with a friend
5. Elsa	5. Safe	5. Got bad news
6. Moana	6. Curious	6. Made a new friend
7. Sponge Bob	7. Lonely	7. Got a new job
8. Darth Vader	8. Confused	8. Moved to a new home
9. Peter Pan	9. Humiliated	9. Was told "no"
10. Barbie	10. Scared	10. Started school
11. Loki	11. Thankful	11. Friend canceled plans
12. Winnie the Pooh	12. Anxious	12. Got a new pet
13. Dory	13. Hesitant	13. Became ill
14. Wonder Woman	14. Relaxed	14. Moved to a new town
15. Harley Quinn	15. Excited	15. Felt hungry
16. The Hulk	16. Furious	16. Got into a car wreck
17. Yoda	17. Strong	17. Got a good night's sleep
18. Buzz Lightyear	18. Upset	18. A family member died
19. The Grinch	19. Frightened	19. Went on a trip
20. Belle	20. Content	20. Was sent to the principal

CANDY LAND: FEELINGS VERSION*

AGES: 5–8   **MODALITY:** INDIVIDUAL, GROUP, FAMILY

Introduction

This is a playful adaptation of the classic board game designed to help children explore emotions, build their feelings vocabulary, and enhance communication by responding to emotion-based prompts as they move across the board. The intervention can provide valuable insights into a client's emotional experiences.

Goals

- Expand feelings vocabulary
- Encourage open communication about emotions
- Gather insights into the client's emotional experiences

Materials

- Candy Land board game
- *Candy Land: Feelings Version Prompts* (provided)

Advance Preparation

- Before the session, if needed, prepare a list of feelings-oriented prompts tailored to the needs of the client(s). Alternatively, you can use the list provided.
- Tip for shorter attention spans: To speed up the game, arrange the Candy Land cards before-hand so that a picture card (typically near the end of the game) is closer to the top of the deck.

Instructions

1. Play Candy Land as normal, with players taking turns picking a card from the deck to indicate where to move their pawn.

2. If the color on the card is different from their pawn's square, or if they pick a picture card, they must answer a question from the list of feelings prompts before moving to the appropriate square on the game board.

3. If the card's color matches their pawn's square, they get to move immediately to that color and get an extra turn without answering a question.

4. Ask process questions such as:
   - What feeling did you like talking about the most?
   - Name a new feeling word that you learned today.
   - Show what you do when you feel angry.

---

* Intervention by Gary G. F. Yorke, PhD

CANDY LAND: FEELINGS VERSION PROMPTS

- All players stand and show what happy looks like with your face and body.

- Say something that makes you happy.

- All players stand and show what sad looks like with your face and body.

- Say something that makes you sad.

- All players stand and show what angry looks like with your face and body.

- Say something that makes you angry.

- All players stand and show what scared looks like with your face and body.

- Say something that makes you scared.

- All players stand and show what excited looks like with your face and body.

- Tell about a time when you felt excited.

- Frustration happens when you're trying to do something difficult and it upsets you. Share a time when you felt frustrated.

- Proud means doing something well. Describe a time when you felt proud.

- Jealousy happens when you feel upset because someone has something you want. Share a time when you felt jealous.

- Disappointment is feeling upset when something doesn't go as expected. Describe a time when you felt disappointed.

- Being brave means doing something even though it's scary. Share a time when you were brave.

FEELINGS DARTS

Introduction

In this dartboard game, clients will have the opportunity to explore and express their feelings in a supportive environment. The game encourages open communication while normalizing the expression of emotions among peers, fostering understanding and emotional growth.

Goals

- Increase open communication regarding feelings
- Gather information about the client

Materials

- *Feelings Darts Prompts* (provided)
- Dartboard and darts (magnetic or foam)
- Paper and writing utensils
- Scissors and a bag or box (optional)
- Small inexpensive prizes (optional)

Advance Preparation

- Create a scorecard that has the name of each player and spaces to add points accumulated during the game.

Instructions

1. The first player takes a turn throwing three darts, noting the total number of points they earned from each space they hit on the board.

2. After the player has thrown the three darts, they choose a question to answer from the list of *Feelings Darts* prompts. Only after providing an appropriate answer to the question do they get awarded the total number of points they earned on the dart board.

3. The game continues until each player has had three turns. At the end of the game, the player with the most total points wins the game (and a prize, if applicable).

4. Encourage discussion among the group by asking follow-up questions throughout the game, such as:
   - What helped you get through that feeling?
   - Who did you talk to about it?
   - What would have made the situation better?
   - Who else here felt the same way?
   - What are some helpful ways you can express or manage this feeling next time it comes up?

Options

- Once a question from the list has been answered, it gets crossed off and cannot be chosen again.
- Each player adds a new question to the game after answering one. The questions must be about feelings and the player can only add a question that they would be willing to answer themselves.
- Cut the questions into paper strips and have the players pull them from a bag or box.

FEELINGS DARTS PROMPTS

- Describe an exciting experience from when you were very young.

- What advice would you give a friend who pretended to be happy, when they actually felt sad?

- Name two things that usually make people feel nervous.

- Who in your family gets angry the most? How do they show their anger?

- When was the last time you felt frustrated? Tell about it.

- What's something that frightens you?

- Tell about a time when a teacher did something that upset you.

- Describe an embarrassing moment.

- Describe something that happened recently that made you laugh.

- Tell about a time when you felt guilty.

- What advice would you give someone who had difficulty expressing anger in appropriate ways?

- Tell about a proud moment from when you were very young.

- Describe a time when a friend disappointed you.

- Tell about a proud moment that happened recently.

- Tell about a time when you had to be brave.

- What advice would you give to a friend who felt lonely?

- Tell about a time when you felt thankful.

- Describe a time when someone in your family made you angry.

- Tell about a time when you felt jealous.

- Describe a time when you appropriately resolved a problem, and how you felt afterward.

FEELING FACE HOP

Introduction

This game aims to increase open communication about feelings and gather valuable insights from the client in a playful manner through physical activity. By hopping onto feeling faces based on their emotions, children can identify and express their emotions more freely.

Goals

- Increase open communication regarding feelings
- Gather information about the client

Materials

- *Feeling Face Hop Questions* (provided)
- Four sheets of paper
- Thick marker

Advance Preparation

- Review the *Feeling Face Hop* questions and modify as needed to fit the child's presenting issues.

Instructions

1. Draw four large feeling faces, each on a separate sheet of paper, along with the corresponding feeling word: *happy*, *sad*, *angry*, and *scared*. Place the four feeling faces on the floor, about two feet apart.

2. Explain to the client that you are going to read some questions to them, and their way of answering will be to jump on the piece of paper that shows their answer. Do a quick test to ensure the client knows what each piece of paper represents.

3. Let them know they can hop on more than one feeling face. For example, if the question is, "Do you feel happy, sad, angry, or scared when someone breaks your favorite toy on purpose?" they might hop on both angry and sad.

4. Begin by asking questions under the level 1 heading. Then move on to the prompts under level 2.

5. Continue the game as needed.

FEELING FACE HOP QUESTIONS

Level 1

Do you feel **happy**, **sad**, **angry**, or **scared** when . . .

- It's your birthday and you get a present

- You wake up from a nightmare

- Your favorite toy breaks

- It's raining so you can't go play outside

- Your parent won't let you have a cookie

- You fall down while playing in the park

- A bee lands on your arm

- Another child pushes you on purpose

- You get a treat

- A dog is barking and growling very loudly

- You get a new toy

Level 2

- Hop on the **happy** face, then tell about a time when you felt a little bit **happy**.

- Hop on the **happy** face, then tell about a time when you felt very **happy**.

- [*Repeat the two questions above with* **sad**, **angry**, *and* **scared**.]

FEELINGS KERPLUNK*

AGES: 7–12   **MODALITY:** INDIVIDUAL, GROUP, FAMILY

Introduction

The playful manner of this game facilitates expression of feelings, develops trust, and helps the child recognize the therapist as a "feeling person" too. The game allows the therapist to observe the client and gather clinical information, and is psychoeducational as the child expands their feelings vocabulary.

Goals

- Increase feelings vocabulary
- Expand therapeutic dialogue about the issues that matter most to the client

Materials

- KerPlunk game
- *Feelings Words* list (provided on page 286)

Instructions

1. Play KerPlunk using the standard rules plus the additional rule that, after each player's turn, the player must choose a feeling from the list and share a time they felt that feeling. Players must choose a different feeling from the list each turn.

2. Play along with consideration of appropriate self-disclosure in mind. The key is to make yourself "human," so try to go beyond superficial and encourage each player to the do same.

3. Be sure to include responses that normalize and validate each player's feelings, such as "Kids your age often tell me they feel..." or "Kids going through divorce have told me that they feel..." or "Sometimes kids feel this way when..."

4. Ask process questions such as:
   - What was the hardest feeling to talk about? The easiest?
   - Which feeling is one you/your family expresses in a healthy way? An unhealthy way?
   - Do you think people can experience more than one feeling at a time?
   - Did you experience any of these feelings while playing KerPlunk? Tell me about it.

---

* Intervention by Janet Vessels, PhD, LPCC-S, RPT-S™

FEELINGS RING TOSS*

AGES: 3–8   **MODALITY:** INDIVIDUAL, GROUP, FAMILY

Introduction

Identifying and discussing feelings can be difficult for some children, especially those who are new to therapy, who have a trauma history, or who tend to internalize their experiences. This game provides a fun and interactive way to help them learn to identify and differentiate emotions while feeling safe and supported. The visual and physical nature of the game makes it easier for children to connect their emotions with facial expressions and situations.

Goals

- Differentiate between four core feelings: happy, sad, angry, and scared
- Match facial expressions with feelings

Materials

- Four sturdy plastic bottles
- Rice, sand, or beans (enough to fill each bottle about one-fourth of the way)
- Funnel
- Masking tape
- *Feelings Faces* handout (provided)
- Four lightweight rings (e.g., clear tubing or paper plates with the centers cut out)
- Scissors
- Colored paper, markers, and other decorative items (optional)

Advance Preparation

- Use a funnel to pour rice, sand, or beans into four clean, dry, label-free bottles, adding just enough weight that they will not tip over. Place the lid on each bottle and secure it with tape so clients cannot open and empty the contents.
- Cut out the feelings faces and tape one to each bottle. (Optional: Wait and invite the client to add the faces and decorate the bottles.)
- Create four lightweight rings that fit over the bottles. You can use clear tubing from a hardware store or cut large holes in the center of paper plates.

Instructions

1. Set the bottles in an open area and place a length of masking tape several feet away.

2. While standing on the taped line, the client takes the four rings, one at a time, and tries to toss them around the bottles. When the client gets a ring around a bottle, they call out the name of the feeling face on that bottle.

---

* Intervention by Pam Dyson, MA, LPC, RPT-S™

3. That feeling is then processed and discussed. For example, you can say to the client, "Share a time when you had that feeling," "What would make a child feel scared?" or "Show me what your face looks like when you're feeling mad." You can also tailor this game to fit specific presenting problems—for example, "What is something that makes you sad about your parents' divorce?"

4. Ask process questions such as:

   - What was the hardest feeling to talk about?

   - How can you handle the frustration when the ring doesn't land on the bottle?

   - Which feeling do you think you experience the most often? Why?

   - Tell about a time when you felt more than one of these feelings at the same time.

FEELINGS FACES

LOLLIPOP TREE

Introduction

This intervention helps young children verbally identify and express a range of emotions while matching these emotions to facial expressions. By engaging in a game, children can develop emotional awareness and communication skills, fostering a better understanding of their own and others' feelings.

Goals

- Verbally identify a range of different emotions
- Match emotions to facial expressions

Materials

- *Lollipop Tree Worksheet* (provided)
- Colored cardboard or construction paper (yellow, blue, red, green, and orange)
- Scissors
- Craft sticks
- Tape
- Crayons (yellow, blue, red, green, and orange)
- Lollipops (one per player)

Advance Preparation

- Make copies of the *Lollipop Tree Worksheet* (one per player).
- Using the colored cardboard or construction paper, cut out five different colored circles (yellow, blue, red, green, and orange). Each circle should be about 3 inches in diameter. Write *happy* on the yellow circle, *sad* on the blue circle, *angry* on the red circle, *scared* on the green circle, and *proud* on the orange circle. Tape each cardboard circle onto a craft stick so they look like lollipops.

Instructions

1. Distribute a *Lollipop Tree Worksheet* to each player, including yourself. Place the five crayons on the table within reach of all the players.

2. Explain the activity. You can use the following script:
   - The Lollipop Tree game will help us talk about feelings. Everyone has feelings. Happy, sad, angry, scared, and proud are some of the ways we sometimes feel.
   - I will pick a colored cardboard lollipop and read the feeling written on it. We will all show with our faces and bodies what that feeling looks like. Then we will take turns telling about a time we experienced that feeling. After sharing, we will color a

lollipop on our paper lollipop tree. We will color the lollipop in the same color as the cardboard lollipop.

- For example, when I pick the yellow cardboard lollipop, we will show what happy looks like with our faces and bodies, then we will take turns telling about a time when we felt happy. We will use the yellow crayon to color in one of the lollipops on our paper lollipop tree.

- We will play the game until we have talked about all five feelings and the five lollipops on our paper lollipop trees have been colored in with the five different colored crayons. Once all the lollipops have been colored in, I have a surprise for you!

3. At the end of the game, distribute a lollipop to each player.

LOLLIPOP TREE WORKSHEET

MANCALA FEELING STONES*

Introduction

This technique provides a safe and structured way for children to express and gauge the intensity of their feelings. It helps them build a deeper understanding of their emotional experiences while also providing a calming, rhythmic activity to promote self-regulation.

Goals

- Increase feelings vocabulary
- Increase open communication regrading feelings

Materials

- Mancala game board
- Stones or large beads in at least four different colors

Instructions

1. Start by having the client sort the colored stones into separate piles. Then assign a feeling to each of the colors (e.g., red = anger, blue = sadness, yellow = happiness, etc.). Depending on the client and presenting issues, you can choose the feelings for them or have them choose.

2. Invite the client to pick a stone representing a feeling they've experienced. For example, if the client selects a red stone to represent anger, they might share, "I felt angry when my mom yelled at me."

3. After the client expresses the feeling, ask them to drop stones into one or more mancala holes to indicate how strong the feeling was. For instance, if they felt mildly angry, they might drop one stone into a hole. If they felt very angry, they might drop several stones into a hole (or many holes), symbolizing greater intensity.

4. Continue this process with each of the emotions identified.

5. Ask process questions such as:
   - Which feeling did you have the most stones for, and why do you think that is?
   - Which feeling was the most difficult to talk about?
   - If you could add a new color of stone for a different feeling, what would it be and why?

---

* Intervention by Tammi Van Hollander, LCSW, RPT-S™

POP IT!

Introduction

This engaging game is designed to help children express their feelings and develop self-regulation skills using Pop Its. Through interactive play, children practice recognizing, labeling, and managing emotions, all while completing playful self-regulation challenges. This group activity fosters communication, emotional awareness, and mindfulness in a safe, supportive setting.

Goals

- Verbally express a range of emotions
- Practice emotional self-regulation techniques

Materials

- Pop Its with at least 20 bubbles (one per player, all the same size and shape)
- Set of at least 15 feelings cards (store bought or written on index cards)
- Paper or whiteboard and a writing utensil
- One standard die

Advance Preparation

- Create at least 15 feelings cards.
- On a whiteboard or piece of paper, create a numbered list of six self-regulation strategies (e.g., take three deep breaths, slowly count to 10, do a quick stretch, name three things you see in the room).
- Optional: Do both tasks with the clients in your group!

Instructions

1. Give each player a Pop It. Spread the feelings cards face down in the center of the table.

2. Invite the first player to begin their turn by rolling the die. The number they roll determines how many bubbles they get to pop on their Pop It.

3. After popping the bubbles, the player draws a feeling card from the pile. They must read the feeling word aloud and share a time when they felt that way. After the player shares, encourage other players to reflect on similar experiences or suggest ways to manage that feeling if it was difficult.

4. The same player rolls the die again. The number they roll corresponds to a self-regulation technique on the list that they must demonstrate for the group.

5. Once the player has finished their self-regulation technique, they pass the turn to the next player.

6. The first player to pop all the bubbles on their Pop It wins the game.

7. Ask process questions such as:

   - What was the most difficult emotion for you to talk about?

   - Which self-regulation technique was your favorite?

   - How do you think practicing these self-regulation techniques can help you manage your feelings outside of the game?

STEPPING STONES*

Introduction

This therapeutic game enhances open communication by encouraging clients to discuss both positive and stressful experiences. By navigating a path made of crumpled and flat pieces of paper, clients will come to understand that everyone encounters both smooth and challenging life events.

Goals

- Increase open communication regarding both positive and stressful experiences
- Normalize that people experience both positive and negative life events

Materials

- Paper

Instructions

1. Create a path on the floor with paper, some crumpled and some laying flat, in a row or a circle. They don't need to be in a specific order or pattern.

2. Have the client start on one end of the path and step to the next piece of paper. Each time they step on a crumpled paper, they share something that was "bumpy" or challenging during the week. Each time they step on a flat piece of paper, they share something that went smoothly or well. They continue until they finish the path.

3. Ask process questions such as:
   - Which type of event—bumpy or smooth—was easier for you to talk about? Why?
   - Did you notice any patterns in the bumpy or smooth parts of your week? How did they affect your mood or behavior?
   - How do you usually handle bumpy moments? What might you try to do differently next time?

---

* Intervention by Batsheva (Beth) Hartstein, LCSW-C, RPT-S™

WHO HAS IT?

Introduction

Helping children identify and verbalize their feelings is crucial for their emotional development and well-being. "Who Has It?" aids this process by engaging children in an interactive game adapted from the familiar children's game "Doggie, Doggie, Where's Your Bone?" It also fosters open communication and helps children develop observation skills, social interaction, and the ability to focus.

Goals

- Verbally identify a range of different emotions
- Increase open communication
- Develop children's observation skills, social interaction, and the ability to focus

Materials

- *Feelings Word Cards* (provided)
- Scissors

Advance Preparation

- Cut out the *Feelings Word Cards* and fold them.

Instructions

1. Choose one player to be the "guesser." The guesser goes out of the room. The rest of the group members sit in a circle.

2. While the guesser is out of the room, choose another player to be the "hider." Give the hider one of the paper feelings words. The hider shares the feeling word with the group and then places it in one of their hands and hides their hands behind their back. All group members also hide their hands behind their backs.

3. Bring the guesser back into the room and have them stand in the middle of the circle. The guesser has two guesses to figure out who has the paper feeling word. Encourage the guesser to pay attention to the body language and facial expressions of the players to help make their guess. The rest of the players can try to trick the guesser by pretending they have the paper feeling word.

4. If the guesser guesses correctly within two tries, then the hider reveals the paper and must tell about a time they felt the feeling depicted on the paper.

5. If the guesser does not guess the hider in two tries, the hider reveals who they are and the feeling word they were hiding. The guesser must then tell about a time they felt the feeling depicted on the paper.

6. Start the next round by identifying the next guesser randomly or by having the current hider become the next guesser. Continue rounds from there.

7. Ask process questions such as:

    - How did you feel when you correctly guessed (or did not correctly guess) the hider?
    - Which was the hardest feeling to talk about?
    - What was a feeling that someone talked about that you have also felt?

WHO HAS IT? FEELINGS WORD CARDS

HAPPY

Something good happens

SAD

Something upsets you

ANGRY

You don't like what happened

SCARED

Something scary or
dangerous is happening

EXCITED

Looking forward to something
good happening

BRAVE

You do something
that's scary to do

FRUSTRATED

You try to do something
but you can't do it

PROUD

You do something very well

CHAPTER 3

Anger, Focus, and Self-Regulation

Children with difficulties in self-regulation, such as those with anger management issues or ADHD, make up a significant portion of referrals to therapy. While some children internalize their anger, becoming depressed or socially withdrawn, many externalize their emotions through aggressive or disruptive behaviors. Whether children are struggling with managing their anger or staying focused, they need practical tools to help regulate their emotional and behavioral responses.

The games in this chapter are designed to help children identify triggers for emotional and behavioral dysregulation, whether rooted in anger or attention deficits such as ADHD. By engaging in these activities, children learn to express anger in constructive ways and build their capacity to focus and sustain attention.

For these strategies to be most effective, it is essential for children to practice new skills both inside and outside the therapy session. Involving parents in the sessions allows them to support their children's progress and reinforce these skills between sessions.

ANGER ICEBERG IN MINECRAFT*

AGES: 7+	**MODALITY:** INDIVIDUAL

Introduction

Incorporating video games into therapy can be an effective way to engage clients by meeting them in the familiar, comfortable environment of a game they enjoy. This approach allows therapists to introduce therapeutic concepts in a setting that feels less formal and more accessible to children and teens. This interactive activity uses the popular game Minecraft to make processing anger more engaging while giving clients a creative way to express what might otherwise be difficult to articulate.

Note: This intervention is for use with children who are familiar with and enjoy using the Minecraft video game. Therapists must be appropriately trained in the use of Minecraft in clinical settings. Using Minecraft as a therapeutic tool is not an official Minecraft product or service, nor is it approved by or associated with Mojang or Microsoft.

Goals

- Identify and label emotions commonly experienced beneath anger (e.g., sadness, loneliness, frustration)
- Express and describe anger effectively
- Gain a deeper understanding of the emotions linked to anger

Materials

- Minecraft licenses for each player
- Computer, games console, or other device with internet access

Advance Preparation

- Be sure the game setting in Minecraft is not "peaceful" so that you can spawn angry or hostile mobs.
- Optional: Build the iceberg ahead of time in Minecraft.
- A helpful video on implementing this intervention is available here: https://www.elliefinch.co.uk/activities

Instructions

1. Introduce the concept of the "anger iceberg," a metaphor that helps people recognize emotions hidden beneath the surface of anger. Explain that this activity will use Minecraft as an interactive way to explore these underlying emotions.

2. Create (or have your client create) an iceberg within Minecraft, either by using ice blocks from the inventory or by finding an existing one in an icy biome (use the command "locate

---

* Intervention by Ellie Finch, MA, MBACP (Accred.)

biome ice plains"). This can be done ahead of time or as part of the activity, depending on your client's comfort level.

3. On top of the iceberg, construct a cage or box out of clear glass blocks. This will be used to contain the mob (symbolizing anger).

4. Ask your client to select a "spawn egg" for a mob from their inventory that represents anger to them (this can be a hostile, passive, or neutral mob). They can choose to either place this mob in the cage to keep it in one place or let it roam free.

5. Beneath the surface of the iceberg (underwater), encourage your client to write or place items or blocks that symbolize emotions that might lie beneath their anger (e.g., loneliness, sadness, frustration). Signs can be used to write emotions, or item frames can be used to place items that represent different feelings. You can pre-place a few items or signs as examples.

   - Which emotions that you have placed beneath the surface surprise you?

   - What other emotions might be beneath your anger?

   - What other mobs might represent anger to you? Why?

   - Would a different mob represent your anger now that you've reflected on it?

   - Now that you've built the iceberg and thought about what lies beneath, do you see the mob you put on top differently? How?

ANGER SPLAT*

AGES: 5+   **MODALITY:** INDIVIDUAL, GROUP, FAMILY

Introduction

This therapeutic game is designed to help children, teens, and families identify and express intensities of their emotions, particularly anger. By using physical activity and visual aids, this game facilitates discussion and understanding of different levels of anger.

Goals

- Understand, identify, and articulate levels of anger in response to various scenarios
- Discuss emotions and appropriate responses to different levels of anger

Materials

- Cotton balls
- Masking tape
- Small container filled with water
- Scissors
- *Anger Splat Labels* (provided)
- *Anger Splat Scenarios* (provided)

Advance Preparation

- Using masking tape, create four square targets, each approximately the size of a piece of printer paper, in a line on a wall. Cut out the *Anger Splat* level labels and tape them next to each target in order of least to most intense.
- Fill a small container with water and place cotton balls nearby, ready for use.

---

* Intervention by Andrea Dorn, MSW, LISW-CP, and Ivey Drawdy, MS, LPC

Instructions

1. Explain that the purpose of the game is to understand and describe the different levels (intensities) of anger. Briefly explore each level to ensure the client understands what each label represents.

Level	Body	Mind
1: Calm/No Anger	I feel peaceful. My muscles are relaxed.	My thoughts are positive or neutral. I am open to new ideas or change.
2: Annoyed/Little Anger	My face or other parts of my body feel warm. My tone of voice is changing.	I am not happy about something or something is bothering me. If it doesn't stop, I may become more angry.
3: Angry/Medium Anger	My heart is beating faster. My muscles are getting tense; my fists are clenching. I may feel like I want to cry or fight. I may raise my voice, roll my eyes, or make other facial expressions.	It's harder to think clearly. I want to act on my feelings. It is challenging to resist expressing my anger.
4: Furious/Big Anger	My muscles are very tense. I cry, fight, or yell. I feel out of control. My angry actions may hurt me, other people, or things. This is the most angry I can feel.	I cannot think clearly. My mind is consumed with angry thoughts. I have to express my anger.

2. Read a scenario prompt aloud to the client. (See the provided *Anger Splat Scenarios* or create your own.) Ask the client to think about a time this scenario has happened to them and how it made them feel. If the scenario hasn't happened to them, then ask how the situation might make them feel.

3. Have the client dip a cotton ball into the water so it is damp, and then throw the damp cotton ball at the target that best represents their level of anger in response to the scenario. Ensure they aim for the square that matches their feelings. The damp cotton ball will stick to the wall where it lands.

4. Depending on time restraints and the age and developmental level of the client, consider asking some of the following questions after each throw:

   - Why did you choose that level?
   - Tell me about a time this happened to you.
   - What about the situation made you feel that way?

- What would have had to happen to make you choose a different anger level in this scenario?
- What other emotions might you feel in this situation?

5. Continue with additional scenario prompts, allowing the client to practice identifying and expressing their anger levels.

6. Once all scenarios have been addressed, reflect on what the client learned about their anger and how they can manage it in the future. Ask questions such as:
   - Which target got the most cotton balls?
   - How do you usually handle this level of anger?
   - What would make you choose a different level of anger in these scenarios?
   - What coping skills could you use to bring your anger level lower in each scenario?

ANGER SPLAT SCENARIOS

Preschool

- Your sibling took your favorite toy without asking.

- You can't have your favorite snack.

- Someone won't play with you.

- It's bedtime and you want to stay up.

- You can't reach something you want.

- Your parent won't let you have a treat.

- You are asked to share your toy when you don't want to.

- Your sibling won't stop copying you, even after you asked them to stop.

- Someone knocks over a block tower you worked hard on.

- Someone says no to something you want.

School-Aged

- Your sibling took your favorite toy without asking.

- You can't figure out your homework and you feel stuck.

- Your parents give you a punishment you don't like.

- You get blamed for doing something you didn't do.

- A friend is spreading a rumor about you.

- Your friend is ignoring you.

- You weren't invited to a classmate's birthday party.

- A classmate takes something from you without asking.

- Someone makes fun of you.

- You're given extra chores when your sibling is not.

Adolescents

- Someone disrespected you or someone you care about.

- Your friend is ignoring you.

- Your parents tell you that you can't go somewhere you really want to go.

- A friend told someone else a secret you shared with them.

- You study hard for a test but still get a bad grade.

- Someone copies your homework and gets a better grade.

- Someone spreads a rumor about you.

- You're excluded from plans with friends.

- Your parents read your private messages without permission.

- Someone bumps into you in the hallway.

LEVEL 1

Calm/No Anger

LEVEL 2

Annoyed/Little Anger

LEVEL 3

Angry/Medium Anger

LEVEL 4

Furious/Big Anger

BANG IT OUT*

Introduction

This game helps children express and regulate their anger in a safe and controlled environment. Using the popular board game Don't Break the Ice as a foundation, this adaptation allows children to verbalize their anger and express the intensity of their feelings through physical actions, promoting self-awareness and emotional regulation.

Goals

- Verbally articulate anger
- Increase the ability to express intensity of anger
- Increase self-regulation

Materials

- Don't Break the Ice board game
- *Anger Scenario Cards* (provided; optional)
- Scissors

Advance Preparation

- Photocopy and cut out the *Anger Scenario Cards* (optional).

Instructions

1. Explain that the purpose of the game is to understand and describe the different levels or intensities of anger.

2. If needed, begin by playing a round of the game following the traditional rules.

3. Then introduce the adapted version of the game: "This time when we play, we will take turns sharing a time when we felt angry. Then we will tap the ice block to show how angry we felt when that event happened. So, if the situation made us feel a little angry, we will tap on the ice cube lightly. If the situation made us feel a lot angry, we will tap on the ice cube harder (but not too hard)." Alternatively, instead of the client coming up with scenarios, use the provided scenario cards.

4. Continue playing the game together, taking turns sharing and tapping the ice cubes accordingly.

5. Provide reflection and validation for the client as they share their experiences with anger. Statements like "Wow, looks like you felt really angry when that happened" or "You were

---

* Intervention by Dr. Fiona Zandt, D.Psych (clinical), RPT™. Adapted with permission from *Creative Ways to Help Children Regulate and Manage Anger: Ideas and Activities for Working with Anger and Emotional Regulation,* by F. Zandt (2024), Jessica Kingsley Publishers.

really angry then; I could see how tight your arms were and I heard your voice get louder" help the client (and their caregivers, if present) increase their awareness of their feelings, including how their anger feels in their body.

6. Ask process questions such as:

- What did you notice about your anger as we played the game?
- What did you notice about your body when you tapped for those big angry feelings? What about the little angry feelings?
- How can you look after yourself when you are feeling angry?

BANG IT OUT ANGER SCENARIO CARDS

You just found out that someone accidentally broke your favorite toy.

You are blamed for something you didn't do, and you feel it's unfair.

It's your birthday and you were really hoping for a specific gift, but you didn't get it.

Someone says something mean to you.

Your sibling accidentally ate the last piece of your favorite snack.

Your best friend forgot to invite you to their birthday party.

Someone cuts in front of you in line when you've been waiting for a long time.

Your friend decides not to let you join a game they are playing.

You were looking forward to going to the park, but it rains and you can't go.

You open your lunch box and discover someone took your snack.

CALMING QUEST: THE LIFE-SIZED ANGER MANAGEMENT GAME*

AGES: 6+   **MODALITY:** INDIVIDUAL, GROUP, FAMILY

Introduction

This game is designed to enhance emotional literacy and self-regulation. It invites participants to build and navigate a life-sized game board, engaging in various therapeutic rules and tasks that promote self-reflection and the practice of calming techniques.

Goals

- Increase emotional literacy and self-reflection of feelings, triggers, and warning signs of anger
- Increase window of tolerance to be able to discuss difficult topics
- Learn, practice, and implement appropriate self-regulation techniques

Materials

- Different colored sheets of paper or floor tiles
- One die
- Optional: materials for "calm down" stations based on coping and calming skills taught in earlier sessions (e.g., bubbles, Hoberman sphere, playdough, fidgets, coloring supplies)

Instructions

1. Explain that you are going to create a life-sized board game about anger where people are the pieces and rules are made up together.

2. Place the pieces of colored paper or floor tiles on the floor (use tape if needed) to create the game board spaces. The path can be straight, curved, or zigzag—whatever works with your space.

3. Create the game rules with the client(s). Examples include:
   - Roll the die and proceed forward that number of spaces.
   - You have to roll a [*specific number*] to start.
   - If you land on [*specific color*] or roll a [*specific number*] you lose a turn.
   - If you roll a [*specific number*] you have to go backward.
   - If you land on [*specific color*] you get an extra turn.

4. Create the "therapy rules" for the game with the client(s). For example, if you roll a [*specific number*] or land on [*specific color*], then:
   - Say something that makes you a little angry.
   - Say something that makes you very angry.

---

* Intervention by Ann Meehan, MS, LPCC, RPT-S™, EMDRIA consultant

- Say one thing you did to relax or calm yourself this week.

- Say one warning sign to anger, such as a thought, body sensation, or behavior.

- Say one thing that used to make you angry but doesn't anymore.

- Share about one time you became angry and successfully used a calming or coping skill.

- Describe one time you saw a character from a TV show, movie, or book get angry.

- You get to ask another player one question related to anger.

5. Optionally, include "calm down stations" with coping and calming skills taught in earlier sessions (e.g., bubbles, Hoberman sphere, playdough, fidgets, coloring). Include this element in your rules—for example, if you land on [*specific color*] or roll a [*specific number*] you take a pause, use one of the calming skills stations, then come back to the game.

6. Optionally, track the intensity of emotions during the game using a subjective units of distress scale (SUDS) and reflecting your observations with the group. If something frustrating happens like going backward, missing a turn, or not being able to start the game, note what you observe (or ask the client to self-assess). If their SUDS level gets over a 6 out of 10, take a calming break together using something from the calming skills station. Consider making the scale a visual tool for everyone in session to see and use.

7. Begin the game by having the first player roll the die. Take turns from there, following the now-created rules as you go.

8. Ask process questions such as:

- How did it feel to physically move along the game board while discussing your emotions?

- Which rule or task did you find most challenging, and why?

- Describe a time during the game when you used a calming skill successfully.

- How did the calming skills stations help you manage your feelings during the game?

- Tell about a situation that might arise in the future when you can use one of the calming skills.

CANDY LAND: SELF-REGULATION VERSION*

Introduction

This version of Candy Land helps young children practice self-regulation techniques while playing a familiar game. Players will engage in role-play and guided prompts to express emotions, such as anger and frustration, and explore healthy ways to manage these feelings. This activity fosters emotional awareness and equips children with tools to handle challenging situations calmly.

Goals

- Verbalize feelings of anger and frustration
- Learn and practice appropriate self-regulation techniques

Materials

- Candy Land board game
- *Candy Land: Self-Regulation Version Prompts* (provided)

Advance Preparation

- Before the session, prepare a list of questions tailored to the needs of the client(s). You can use the examples from the *Candy Land: Self-Regulation Version Prompts* list included at the end of this activity.

Instructions

1. Set up the Candy Land board in the usual way.

2. Players take turns picking a card from the deck. If the color on the card is different from their pawn's square or if they pick a picture card, they must answer a self-regulation question before moving to the appropriate square on the game board. If the card's color matches their pawn's square, they move immediately to that color and get an extra turn without answering a question.

3. Alternate version: Whenever the players land on a square that is the same color as their pawn, they must answer a question.

4. Ask processing questions such as:
   - What is something you learned from this game?
   - How did it feel to practice staying calm when something didn't go your way?
   - What was the hardest part of the game for you, and how did you handle it?
   - What can you do differently next time you feel angry or frustrated?

---

* Intervention by Gary G. F. Yorke, PhD

CANDY LAND: SELF-REGULATION VERSION PROMPTS

- What makes you a little angry? What makes you very angry?

- When something gets too hard, some people get angry or frustrated. It can help to take a break and count to ten. All players practice doing this now.

- Some people like to laugh at other people. Say, "Please stop laughing at me. That hurts my feelings."

- Pretend your parent sent you to your room for ten minutes because you misbehaved. Show what it looks like to sit calmly and quietly.

- Pretend someone is teasing you and they won't stop. Name an adult who can help you.

- Pretend you're going to hit someone. Say "no hitting," and walk to the other side of the room.

- Pretend you are very angry. All players take a deep breath in for three seconds, then slowly blow the anger out for four seconds.

- Pretend someone grabbed your toy. Practice saying calmly and nicely, "That's mine. Please give it back."

- Pretend you just turned over the Gingerbread Man card and you have to go all the way back to that space and you're going to lose the game. Show an appropriate way to handle this.

COUNT THE CARDS*

Introduction

This game helps enhance attention span and focus by having clients practice blocking out nonessential stimuli and maintaining concentration on a specific task. By navigating distractions and maintaining focus on counting cards, participants develop essential skills for better attention and concentration in various aspects of their lives.

Goals

- Increase attention span
- Increase ability to focus
- Practice blocking out nonessential stimuli

Materials

- Standard 52-card deck

Instructions

1. Ask the client if they ever get distracted, especially when they're supposed to be focusing. Have the client generate a list of situations that require intense focus (e.g., taking a test, trying to win a video game, using scissors). Then have the client generate another list of the kinds of situations that tend to distract them from their tasks (e.g., loud noises, someone teasing them, phones or screens, others playing when they are working).

2. Take the deck of cards and count them continuously aloud once from 1 to 52. Then ask, "Not too hard, right? What if there are things around me that are distracting me from counting the cards—would that make it easier or harder?"

3. Instruct the client to count the cards continuously aloud from 1 to 52. They must keep their eyes on the deck of cards the whole time. They cannot stop counting or take their eyes off the cards. When they get to 52, they win.

4. While the client is counting, you (and the caregiver or other group members, if present) do and say things to distract the card counter, to interrupt the counting, or to get them to look up from the cards. Participants cannot touch the card counter or use curse words. The client must focus on counting and block out the distractions in order to successfully count the cards.

5. The client may not succeed the first time. The game should be repeated until the client (and each group member) has had a successful turn.

---

* Intervention by Paris Goodyear-Brown, LCSW, RPT-S™

6. Ask process questions such as:
   - How did it feel to try to count while others were distracting you?
   - What skills did you use to stay focused on the task of counting the cards?
   - How did it feel to accomplish the task of staying focused to count the cards?
   - When are other times in your life you need to concentrate on a specific task?

7. Encourage the client and their caregiver to practice focusing at home. The caregiver can blast the TV or bang pots and pans while the client is trying to do their homework. The client must ignore the caregiver's attempts to distract them and complete their work.

DICE MOVES*

AGES: 7–12   **MODALITY:** INDIVIDUAL, GROUP

Introduction

This game is designed to help clients practice focusing by asking them to move only certain parts of their body at a time. Depending on what is rolled, the player may be moving one part of their body, one half of their body, or one side of their body. The primary motor cortex on the left side of the brain controls movement on the right side of the body and vice versa. Practicing this can help with mindfulness skills that can be used in all areas of life.

Goals

- Increase ability to focus
- Learn about and practice the concepts of mindfulness

Materials

- One standard die
- Timer

Instructions

1. Explain: "Mindfulness means paying full attention to what you're doing right now and noticing how you feel. It requires mindfulness to focus on moving only certain parts of your body, which is what this game is about."

2. Players take turns being the leader. The leader rolls the die to determine which part of the body the group members will move: 1 = hands, 2 = feet, 3 = upper half, 4 = lower half, 5 = left half, and 6 = right half. Then the leader decides how to move that part, such as flapping, doing circles in the air, bending, or shaking.

3. Set a timer for 20 seconds (or another amount; it should be challenging but not impossible). The other players follow the leader's movements until the timer goes off, trying not to think about anything else other than the part of their body that they are moving and how they are moving.

4. Play on from here, having the players take turns being the leader.

5. Ask process questions such as:
   - How did you feel in your body before/during/after playing?
   - When did you have to focus the most?
   - Were you thinking about anything else when performing these moves? If not, then you experienced mindfulness!
   - Where else in your life can you use mindfulness skills?

---

* Intervention by Tracey Turner-Bumberry, LPC, RPT-S™, CAS

FAST BALL, SLOW BALL*

AGES: 4–8   **MODALITY:** INDIVIDUAL

Introduction

This game emphasizes the crucial skill for young children of understanding their emotions and responding appropriately to different situations. Through a fun and interactive game of rolling a ball at different speeds, children learn to identify how their bodies feel in moments of excitement or calm, express a range of emotions, and practice coping strategies to regulate their feelings effectively.

Goals

- Establish an ability to focus on body cues to identify when regulation is needed
- Learn and practice how to cope with feelings in the moment
- Increase frustration tolerance

Materials

- Ball
- Timer

Instructions

1. Explain to the client that you are going to play a game to see how many times the two of you can roll the ball back and forth to each other within a given time frame.

2. Engage the client in a competitive and fun game to get the highest amount of rolls in a given time on the timer. After a few rounds, pause the game and ask the client how they are feeling, including how they are feeling in their body (e.g., heart rate increasing, sweating, excited, anxious).

3. Now change the game to seeing how *slowly* you can roll the ball back and forth to each other to get the *least* amount of completed rolls within a given time frame. After a few rounds, pause the game and ask the client how they are feeling, including how they are feeling in their body (e.g., decreased heart rate, bored, frustrated, tired).

4. Discuss the difference in feelings between the two versions of the game and compare this to feelings they experience in their lives. For example, what feelings do they have when life is "fast" and what feelings do they have when life is "slow"?

5. Resume the game, but this time have the client lead when to go slower or faster based on their feeling of when the game is getting too fast or slow. After a few rounds, ask the client for ideas on how to regulate to go slower when they feel things are moving too fast. Explore with the client what coping strategies can be used to go from moving "faster" to "slower" in their everyday life and practice these within the game.

---

* Intervention by Lynette Nikkel, MSW, RSW

6. Ask processing questions such as:

- How did your body feel when we were playing the game at a fast speed? What changes did you notice in your heart rate or energy level?

- When we switched to playing the game slowly, how did your body and emotions feel? Did you find it harder or easier to stay calm?

- When life feels fast or overwhelming, what are some things you can do to slow down and help your body feel calm again?

FAST PLAY, SLOW PLAY*

AGES: 6–12   **MODALITY:** INDIVIDUAL

Introduction

This modified version of the classic memory matching game helps the client experience the consequences of inattentive, impulsive behavior versus the benefits of focused, controlled behavior.

Goals

- Explore the consequences of impulsive and inattentive behavior
- Increase attention span, impulse control, and self-control

Materials

- Memory game or standard 52-card deck
- Paper and writing utensils

Advance Preparation

- If using a standard card deck, divide the cards into two sets of matching pairs (one for each round of the game).

Note: Some children can become frustrated with this type of activity, so it is important to introduce the game in a playful and engaging manner and reinforce that the purpose is to practice moving too fast and practice moving slowly to understand the difference and develop strategies to develop more control. Since you are playing alongside the client, you can model the process.

Instructions

1. Play a round of the classic memory matching game with the client, but explain that you both must turn over the cards as quickly as possible, without thinking about which cards to turn or trying to remember where the matches are located.

2. After the game is played using this format, discuss how mistakes were made and successful matching of pairs was difficult due to the inattentive, impulsive behavior you both exhibited.

3. Play the game a second time with the remaining set of matching pairs. This time, explain that you will both concentrate and use strategy prior to turning cards over. As a result, you should experience more success at obtaining matches because you are focusing your attention and controlling your behavior as opposed to impulsively turning over cards.

---

* Intervention by Sueann Kenney-Noziska, MSW, LCSW, RPT-S™

4. Discuss the consequences of playing fast and haphazardly versus the benefits of a slow and controlled approach. Specific strategies the client utilized during the "slow play" round should be identified and discussed. Generalization of these skills and strategies should be conducted. Ask questions such as:

   - What did you notice about your ability to find matching pairs?
   - What strategies did you use to help you concentrate and remember where the cards were during the slow play?
   - What did you learn about the difference between acting impulsively and taking your time to think things through?
   - How can you use the strategies you learned from the game in other situations, like at school or at home?

5. As the strategies are identified, write them on a piece of paper. The client can then decorate the paper to create a poster of strategies they can use to remain attentive and controlled. The poster serves as a transitional object and a strategy to increase generalization of the skills identified through the technique. The poster can be reviewed with the caregiver at the end of the session. The caregiver should be encouraged to reinforce and model the strategies in between sessions.

FISHING FOR COPING SKILLS*

Introduction

This game helps clients identify and recognize appropriate coping strategies they can use in response to various stressful situations. The fishing element makes it interactive and engaging, promoting hands-on learning and retention.

Goals

- Identify and apply effective coping skills for various stressors
- Improve problem-solving and critical thinking skills by identifying which coping skill is an appropriate response to a given stressful situation

Materials

- Fishing pole (stick with a string and a magnet on the end)
- Magnets or paper clips
- *Stressful Situation Cards* (provided)
- *Coping Skills Cards* (provided)
- Scissors
- Container or blue cardboard/construction paper

Advance Preparation

- Print and cut out the provided situation cards and coping skills cards. Also make some blank cards for clients to add their own stressors and coping strategies.
- Attach a magnet or paper clip to each coping skill card.
- Place the coping skills cards face down in a container (or cut a piece of blue cardboard or construction paper to make a pond).
- Lay the stressor cards face down beside the pond.

Instructions

1. Discuss what stressful situations are and introduce the concept of coping skills. Give examples of stressors (e.g., feeling left out at school, finding your sibling's behavior annoying) and coping skills (e.g., talking to a trusted adult, taking deep breaths).

2. Explain that the goal of the game is to match stressful situations with the best coping strategies using the magnetic fishing pole.

3. The client randomly chooses a situation card and reads it out loud. Then they "fish" a coping skill card from the pond and read that card out loud.

---

* Intervention by Holly Willard, LCSW, RPT-S™

4. The client then decides whether the coping skill they caught would be effective for the situation. If the coping skill card is a good match for the situation, the client places it next to the situation card and explains why they believe it would help. If it does not match the situation, the client places it back in the pond and continues fishing until they find an appropriate coping strategy for the situation.

5. Optional: For each matched coping skill, role-play the scenario with the client to practice using the strategy.

6. Continue playing until the client has matched a coping skill to each identified situation.

7. Consider having the client create their own situation cards based on real-life experiences or think of additional coping strategies to add to the pond for future rounds.

8. Ask process questions such as:
   - How did it feel to find the right coping skill for each stressor?
   - What coping strategies will you try using more often?"
   - How could using these strategies change the way you handle stressful situations?

9. Carry this intervention over to subsequent sessions by discussing the client's experience using these coping skills. For example, ask them what worked and what didn't. Explore new strategies or refine existing ones based on their experiences.

FISHING FOR COPING SKILLS: STRESSFUL SITUATION CARDS

You see your friends playing together and they didn't invite you. You feel left out.	You receive a lower grade than expected on a test.
You and a friend had a disagreement and aren't talking to each other.	You're feeling like no one understands you.
You have a lot of homework to do and don't know where to start.	You did something wrong, and now you're worried about getting in trouble.
Someone at school is making fun of you and calls you a mean name.	You have an important test coming up, and you're feeling nervous.
You did something embarrassing in front of your friends.	You have to go to a new place, and you feel nervous about it.
Your parents ask you to stop playing a video game, but you are in the middle of an important part.	Your sibling is being annoying and you want to hit them.

FISHING FOR COPING SKILLS: COPING SKILLS CARDS

Take three slow, deep breaths in through your nose and out through your mouth.	Count slowly from 1 to 10 to calm your mind and body.
Walk away from the situation.	Draw or write what you are feeling.
Find an adult you trust and tell them what's bothering you.	Listen to music.
Say something positive to yourself, like "I can handle this."	Do physical activity like running, jumping jacks, or stretching.
Watch a funny video or think of something that makes you laugh.	Identify three things you see around you to distract yourself from the upsetting feelings.
Ask for them to stop and if they don't, find a trusted adult to help.	Express your feelings and try to find a compromise.

EMOTIONAL FREEZE DANCE*

Introduction

This engaging activity helps children practice emotional expression and enhance their focus and impulse control. By combining music and movement with emotions, children learn to express different feelings using their face and body, improving their emotional awareness and regulation skills in an engaging and interactive way.

Goals

- Practice emotional expression by showing how different emotions are expressed through the face and body
- Improve focus and impulse control

Materials

- Music
- Index cards and a writing utensil

Advance Preparation

- Create game cards with feelings written on them (e.g., excited, angry, sad, proud, scared, disgusted, calm, frustrated, confused, loved).

Instructions

1. Place the game cards face up on a table.

2. Explain: "This game is like freeze dance, but we are going to use emotions. I will pick a game card that has an emotion written on it. I will start the music and you will start dancing. Then I will stop the music and call out the emotion written on the card (instead of "Freeze!") and you will stop dancing. When the music starts again, you will dance using your face and body to express that emotion until the music stops again and I call out another emotion for you to demonstrate while dancing. We will play a few rounds."

3. Afterward, ask process questions such as:
   - How did it feel to express different emotions through your body and face during the game?
   - Were there any emotions that were challenging to express? How did you manage to show them?
   - Was it easy or difficult to stop dancing when the music stopped?
   - How can you use what you learned in this game in your everyday life when you feel these emotions?

---

* Intervention by Lauren Mosback, LPC, NCC

FREEZIES

AGES: 5–10   **MODALITY:** INDIVIDUAL, GROUP, FAMILY

Introduction

This game strengthens self-regulation skills and increases the ability to focus for longer periods. By engaging in fun and interactive activities that require them to periodically freeze and stay still, children can practice and enhance their self-control and concentration in a playful context.

Goals

- Strengthen self-regulation skills
- Develop ability to focus for increasingly longer periods of time

Materials

- A ball that is soft, no bigger than a volleyball
- Two Pop It fidget toys that are exactly the same size
- Bubbles

Instructions

1. There are several versions of the Freezies game. The client can choose in which order to play them:

   - **Basketball Freezies:** If in a group, divide into pairs. Take turns making a basketball hoop with your arms, while the other player throws the ball to try to get it through the hoop. Each time the player gets a basket, the player must freeze (stand completely still) for 10 seconds. Players earn one point if they freeze for 10 seconds, and two points if they freeze for 20 seconds.

   - **Pretend Freezies:** Participants pretend to be something that moves (e.g., airplane, bunny, marching soldier) until the leader says "Freezies!" and all must freeze (stand completely still) for 10 seconds. Play additional rounds taking turns being the leader and pretending to be different things.

   - **March! Hop! Clap! Freezies:** Participants must follow the leader's command. When the leader says "March!" participants must march around the room. When the leader says "Hop!" participants must hop around the room. When the leader says "Clap!" participants must clap their hands. When the leader says "Freezies!" participants must freeze (stand completely still). Take turns being the leader.

   - **Freeze-Off:** Pairs stand back to back. At the count of three, turn toward each other and freeze (stand completely still). See who can freeze the longest.

   - **Popcorn Freezies:** Participants squat, pretending they are a kernel of popcorn. The leader counts. When the leader says the number 10, all participants jump up and "pop," then freeze (stand completely still) for 10 seconds.

- **Pop It Freezies:** This involves two competing players, who get identically sized Pop It fidget toys. One player is designated as the leader (or a third person who is not playing could be the leader). Both competing players count down: "Three, two, one, go!" at which point they begin to pop as many bubbles on their Pop Its as they can. Whenever the leader says "Freezies!" both players must freeze (stand completely still) for 10 seconds, then resume popping. The player who pops all the bubbles on their Pop It is the winner. (To make the game more challenging, players can only use one finger to pop the bubbles.)
- **Bubble Freezies:** The leader blows bubbles. Participants must pop as many as they can until the leader says "Freezies!" then all must freeze. You can add rules to make the game more challenging (e.g., players can only pop bubbles with their pinky/foot/elbow).

2. Ask process questions such as:

- How did it feel to freeze?
- What skills did you use to freeze?
- When are other times in your life you need to freeze or sit still, and how can you use the strategy from these games in those situations?

THE GAME ABOUT NOTHING

AGES: 6+   **MODALITY:** INDIVIDUAL, GROUP, FAMILY

Introduction

This intervention, ideally for use in family sessions, helps clients learn and practice appropriate self-calming strategies when feeling angry or frustrated. By engaging in scenarios that trigger frustration and practicing the "nothing" technique, participants can develop effective problem-solving skills and enhance emotional regulation.

Note: While this activity is appropriate for individual and group sessions (with some modifications to the steps), it is most effective for family therapy.

Goals

- Learn, practice, and implement appropriate self-calming strategies when feeling angry
- Strengthen problem-solving skills

Materials

- At least 20 index cards in two colors (at least 10 of each color)
- Writing utensil

Advance Preparation

- Prepare game cards by writing scenarios that typically trigger feelings of anger or frustration on the index cards. Ensure the scenarios are appropriate to the client's age and circumstances. Prepare at least 10 cards for the child (using one color of index cards) and at least 10 cards for the caregivers (using the other color). Keep the two sets of cards separate. Leave some cards blank for the clients to add their own scenarios.
- Here are some examples:

Scenario Cards for Children

- You lose a game.
- Your parent won't buy you a treat.
- Your sibling grabs the remote from you.
- Your sibling gets a bigger piece of cake.
- Your drawing didn't come out well.
- You don't understand your homework.
- Your teacher scolded you in front of the class.
- Your friend broke a toy you lent them.
- You were told to turn off your video game before finishing a level.
- Your sibling accidentally spilled juice on your homework.

Scenario Cards for Caregivers

- ○ Your child ignores you when you ask them to brush their teeth.
- ○ Your child is throwing a tantrum because you won't give them a cookie.
- ○ You're having trouble opening a jar of jam.
- ○ Your children are fighting over which TV show to watch.
- ○ You overcooked your dinner.
- ○ Your child refuses to do their homework.
- ○ You received a call from the school about your child's behavior.
- ○ Your partner is late coming home, and dinner is getting cold.
- ○ You misplaced your keys and are running late for an appointment.
- ○ You found a mess in the living room that your children didn't clean up.

Add more complex scenarios for older children or families that include multiple steps or problem-solving components. For example, "You have a big school project due tomorrow, and your sibling is being loud and distracting you."

- Meet with the caregivers prior to the family session. Discuss validation as an appropriate way for them to respond to their child's anger (e.g., "I can see that you're angry because I won't buy you a treat").

- Teach the caregivers the concept of co-regulation, then role-play to facilitate mastery. You can say, "Co-regulation is when a caregiver supports their child in managing their emotions by staying calm and providing comfort and guidance or modeling calm behavior themselves. It's like being an anchor for your child when they're feeling overwhelmed, helping them feel safe and regulated. When you stay calm, you create a space where your child can learn how to calm down and manage their emotions too."

Instructions

1. Begin the family session by explaining: "Today I am going to teach you something very important. I'm going to teach you [*pause for three seconds*] . . . nothing! You heard me correctly—I am going to teach you . . . nothing! Here's how to do . . . nothing! [*Stand silently and simply breathe for 10 seconds.*] What did you notice me doing?" The child might say something like "You were just standing there." Respond by saying, "That's right, I was just standing there doing . . . nothing!"

2. Invite the caregivers to do the "nothing" technique (stand silently and simply breathe for 10 seconds). Praise them by saying "Good job doing nothing!" Then invite the child to try the technique, and prompt the caregivers to praise the child by saying "Good job doing nothing!"

3. Brainstorm appropriate ways to handle situations that trigger anger or frustration, such as self-talk or calmly talking about feelings.

4. Introduce the game:
   - Now that you are experts at doing nothing and you have learned some appropriate ways to handle your anger, you're ready to play the "nothing" game. You will take turns picking a game card. [*Indicate which stack is for the child and which is for the caregivers.*]
   - These cards have situations that typically make people angry written on them. You will pretend that you are in that situation, and instead of reacting to it by having an anger outburst, you will practice the nothing technique. Remember, this means standing silently and doing nothing except breathing for 10 seconds. Then you will say an appropriate way to handle the situation. The purpose is to calm your anger by doing the nothing technique so you can then think more clearly and come up with a better way to manage your feelings.
   - You earn one point each time you do the nothing technique correctly, plus a bonus point for coming up with an appropriate way to calmly handle the situation. Let's see how many points you can get!

5. Optional round: Include a role-reversal segment where the child and caregivers switch roles and draw cards from the other's pile. This helps build empathy and understanding of each other's perspectives.

6. *Ask process questions such as:*
   - How can the nothing technique help you?
   - How can the nothing technique help your family?
   - How will you feel if your home is more calm?
   - Are there situations where the nothing technique is not appropriate? (For example, if a child is hitting their sibling, a more appropriate caregiver response would be to calmly intervene to stop the hitting, then enforce an appropriate consequence for the hitting, such as no screen time for 24 hours.)

7. Encourage the family to implement the nothing technique at home. Suggest that caregivers come up with a signal to prompt their child to use the nothing technique when they feel angry, such as holding up two fingers to make a peace sign.

LET'S PLAY BALL

AGES: 4–8   **MODALITY:** INDIVIDUAL, GROUP

Introduction

This therapeutic game helps children develop self-regulation through a series of playful and interactive activities using a simple soft ball. The activities encourage focus, self-control, and understanding the importance of following rules. In this way, children learn essential skills for emotional and behavioral regulation while having fun.

Goals

- Improve self-regulation
- Articulate the value of following rules during gameplay

Materials

- Soft ball that is easy for young children to catch

Instructions

1. Explain that this game is a fun way to work on focus, self-control, and following the rules of a game.

2. If in a group session, have everyone form a circle at a distance where they can easily toss the ball to each other. Otherwise, simply face the client at a good range.

3. Play several rounds of the game as follows:

   - **Round 1—Eye Contact Toss:** Players take turns throwing the ball to others. They must make eye contact with the person they are throwing to. After a few tosses, ask the children how it felt to keep eye contact while throwing the ball. Was it easy or hard to focus on both the ball and the person?

   - **Round 2—Slow Toss for Self-Control:** Players throw the ball to others very slowly, trying to control their movements and avoid rushing. Then discuss how it felt to throw the ball slowly. Did they want to throw it faster? What helped them control that urge?

   - **Round 3—Quick Toss for Focus:** Players throw the ball to others quickly, but with control! The focus is on keeping concentration and not letting the ball drop, even as the pace increases. Then ask how they felt when the ball was moving quickly. Was it hard to stay focused? What helped them?

   - **Round 4—Managing Distraction Challenge:** One player throws the ball up in the air 10 times, counting each toss out loud (1 to 10). Meanwhile, the other players count backward from 10 to 1, trying to distract the first player. Process by asking the player throwing the ball how it felt to focus with distractions. For the distracting players, ask what they noticed about how the first player managed to focus.

- **Round 5—Break the Rules:** One player will break a "ball play" rule (such as hogging the ball instead of throwing it) on purpose. Then ask everyone how it felt when the rule was broken, and why we have rules when playing games like this.
- **Round 6—Teamwork Toss:** Everyone must work together to toss the ball from player to player for as long as possible, counting each toss. If the ball drops, they start over and try to beat their previous record. Process by asking how it felt to work together.

4. After completing all the rounds, ask additional process questions such as:
   - Which round of the game was your favorite? Why do you think that is?
   - Are there areas of your life where focusing, managing distractions, teamwork, and rule following are helpful?

TARGETING ANGER*

Introduction

This game provides an engaging way to help children recognize anger triggers and learn coping skills. Combining the physical act of throwing a ball with verbal discussion increases the opportunity for integration. The kinesthetic and experiential nature of the game makes it ideal for younger children with limited attention spans. The playful, hands-on learning optimizes motivation and generalization of skills outside the therapy room.

Goals

- Identify anger triggers
- Scale the intensity of angry feelings
- Learn appropriate strategies for managing anger

Materials

- Velcro ball and target set (the style with a numbered dartboard)
- Sticky notes and writing utensil

Instructions

1. Practice playing the game as intended, aiming to stick the ball as close to the center as possible.

2. Then invite the client to notice the numbers on the board. Ask, "Which numbers were the hardest to hit—the larger or smaller numbers?" (The higher the numbers get on the board, the harder they are to hit.) Explain to the client: "Our anger also comes in different sizes. Something might make us a little angry, medium angry, or very angry. The bigger the angry feelings, the more difficult it can be to manage. We can become of aware of what makes us angry and use our coping skills to target it before it gets too big. Let's give it a try!"

3. Players resume throwing the ball at the target. This time, however, when they hit a number, they must identify an angry event that corresponds to the size of that number: small, medium, or large (e.g., "I felt medium angry when my brother took my toy!") They will then write down on a sticky note a coping skill that would help with anger this size (e.g., taking deep breaths) and post it on the board. (For more examples of coping skills, see the list provided on page 290.)

4. After each player has taken a turn adding a coping skill to the board, say, "Imagine that this ball represents our angry feelings. Sometimes when we get really angry we can feel overwhelmed. Our anger can feel struck, just like this ball gets stuck to the dartboard. This doesn't feel good!" Invite the child pull the Velcro ball off the board and continue explaining: "But when we add our coping skills, the ball just bounces off the pieces of paper without

---

* Intervention by Sheri Eggleton, Hons. RP, CTIC

getting stuck. Coping skills can act like a shield that prevents our anger from getting stuck and getting too big."

5. Continue to play the game, with the goal of filling the board with coping skills until the anger will no longer get stuck.

6. Ask process questions such as:

    - What did you notice when you played the game before adding the coping skills? After?

    - How did the number of coping skills affect the game?

    - What do you think this means for managing angry feelings?

    - Which coping skills work best for you when you feel angry? Tell about a time you used one of these skills.

    - Did you learn about any new coping skills that you would like to try? When could you use these skills?

MINDFUL BALLOON FREEZE DANCE*

Introduction

This activity combines engaging physical movement with mindful breathing exercises to help participants learn emotional regulation and effective stress management techniques. Through dancing and intentional breathing, this group or family activity fosters stronger relationships, enhances attunement among participants, and increases present-moment awareness, promoting a calmer and more focused state of mind.

Goals

- Strengthen relationships by building attunement and engagement
- Teach emotional regulation and effective breathing techniques to manage anger and stress, promoting regulation and mindfulness
- Increase present-moment awareness

Materials

- Music
- Balloon

Instructions

1. Start by teaching deep breathing: "Inhale deeply through your nose for three seconds, then exhale slowly through your mouth for four seconds."

2. Explain: "When we are angry, it is hard to think clearly because there is not enough oxygen going into our brains. We might say or do something that we don't mean. Deep, slow breathing quiets our minds so we have space to make an appropriate choice. We also know that co-regulation calms our nervous systems. This means that when we come together and take deep breaths, we can better regulate our minds and bodies. Let's practice by playing a game together with a balloon."

3. Have one player select the music to be played while you manage the pause button.

4. When the music starts, the players dance together, gently tapping the balloon back and forth to each other, trying to keep it in the air. When the music stops, the closest person catches the balloon.

5. Everyone in the group then gathers around that person, putting one hand on the balloon. Together they inhale deeply through their nose, raising the balloon above their heads. They then exhale slowly through their mouths while lowering the balloon. Do this two to three times, encouraging them to watch each other closely and notice each other's breath and

---

* Intervention by Tammi Van Hollander, LCSW, RPT-S™

movement. Challenge them to keep the balloon from hitting the ground during their collective breathing.

6. Start the next round by restarting the music, at which time all group members let the balloon go and resume gently tapping it to keep it in play. Play several rounds, giving each member a turn to choose the dance song.

7. Optional: As an added challenge, encourage silly and exaggerated dance moves that might make it more difficult to focus on keeping the balloon in the air.

8. Ask process questions such as:
   - How did it feel to work together to keep the balloon in the air?
   - Give an example of a time when it can help you to do deep breathing.
   - How did it feel when the music stopped? Which was more fun?
   - Was there a time in the game that felt challenging? What about a time when you felt successful?
   - Did you like breathing together with the balloon or would you have liked to take deep breaths on your own?
   - How was it working with others to keep the balloon in play?

MUSIC MADNESS

AGES: 4–7   **MODALITY:** GROUP, FAMILY

Introduction

This adaptation of musical chairs is designed to help young clients learn about and practice self-calming strategies when they are feeling angry or frustrated. Through movement, music, and calming exercises, children can identify feelings of anger and frustration while learning how to manage these emotions effectively.

Goals

- Identify situations that cause feelings of anger or frustration
- Learn, practice, and implement an appropriate calming strategy when feeling angry or frustrated

Materials

- Music player and music
- Colored cardstock or construction paper (one piece fewer than there are players)

Instructions

1. Begin by teaching and practicing three different calming strategies (for ideas, see the list of coping skills provided on page 290).

2. Place the colored paper in random spots on the floor, keeping about three feet between each one.

3. Play the music and instruct the players to dance around the room, making sure they don't step on any of the papers on the floor. When the music stops, everyone quickly tries to find a paper on the floor and stand on it.

4. Like musical chairs, there is always one less spot than there are players, so one person is left without a paper to stand on. That player must choose one of the three self-calming strategies to do.

5. Play several rounds of the game.

6. Ask process questions such as:
   - How did it feel when you couldn't find a paper to stand on?
   - Which calming strategy is your favorite?
   - What did you notice about your body or your breathing when you used a calming strategy?
   - Think of a time when using a calming strategy could help you.

NATURE PEEK AND SEEK*

Introduction

This activity is designed to help children connect with nature while improving their focus, concentration, and working memory. The game involves identifying nature items hidden under a blanket, encouraging both memory skills and exploration as the child searches for similar items in the natural environment.

Goals

- Establish positive connection with nature
- Improve focus, concentration, and working memory

Materials

- Access to an outdoor space
- Several nature items (e.g., leaf, acorn, flower, pine cone)
- Blanket or towel
- Timer
- Camera

Instructions

1. Explain: "This game will help you have fun in nature and improve your concentration and memory. I have placed several nature items underneath this blanket. I will lift up the blanket for one minute for you to take a quick peek at the items. I will then cover them back up with the blanket and you will go look around our nature area and seek as many of these nature items that you can find in five minutes. You can take a picture of the item or, if you find it on the ground, you can bring it back to this area. After the time is up, we will see how many items you found that match what is under the blanket. Now, let's peek!"

2. The number of items can be increased or decreased as needed to make the game more or less challenging.

3. Ask process questions such as:
   - How did it feel to explore nature and try to remember the items under the blanket?
   - What strategy did you use to recall and find the nature items?
   - How can you use this strategy to focus or concentrate at school or when doing your homework?

---

* Intervention by Jamie Lynn Langley, LCSW, RPT-S™. Adapted with permission from "Nature Play Therapy as a Healing Way for Children, Teens, and Families: Incorporating Nature with Play and Expressive Therapies," by J. L. Langley, in J. A. Courtney, J. L. Langley, L. L. Wonders, R. Heiko, & R. LaPiere (Eds.), *Nature-Based Play and Expressive Therapies: Interventions for Working with Children, Teens, and Families* (2022), Routledge.

NO BIG DEAL

AGES: 8–12   **MODALITY:** INDIVIDUAL, GROUP, FAMILY

Introduction

This therapeutic game helps children distinguish between situations that warrant strong emotional reactions (big deals) and those that do not (no big deals). It aims to teach children the valuable skill of emotional regulation, promoting healthier responses to everyday challenges.

Goals

- Distinguish between situations that warrant strong emotional reactions and those that do not
- Implement appropriate emotional responses and coping strategies

Materials

- *Situation Cards*, *Coping Chart*, and *Practice Sheet* (provided)
- Scissors
- Large sheet of paper
- Marker
- Tape

Advance Preparation

- Make a copy of the *Situation Cards*, *Coping Chart*, and *Practice Sheet*. Cut out the cards and create a few blank cards for the client to add their own situations later.

Instructions

1. Draw a line down the middle of a large sheet of paper. On the top left, write "BIG DEAL." On the top right, write "NO BIG DEAL." Tape the sheet to the wall.

2. Explain to the client that you're going to play a game to learn the difference between a "big deal" and "no big deal." Use examples from the child's life to illustrate both concepts.

3. Instruct the client to draw a situation card and read it out loud. Discuss whether the situation is a big deal or no big deal. Use tape to stick the card on the appropriate side on the chart.

4. If the situation is no big deal, the client must say to themselves, "It's no big deal." If the situation is a big deal, then the client chooses an appropriate coping strategy from the coping chart.

5. Optional: Have the client role-play the scenario, using the coping strategy. After the role-play, reflect on how the situation was handled.

6. Continue playing with the remaining cards and encourage the client to add their own situation cards to the game.

7. Provide the client with the practice sheet and the coping chart to take home. Encourage them to use the "no big deal" strategy when they encounter a situation that is no big deal and one of the strategies from the coping chart when faced with a situation that is a big deal.

8. Ask process questions such as:
   - Tell about a time when you had an anger outburst about a situation that you now realize was a "no big deal."
   - How could saying to yourself, "It's no big deal" help you?
   - What advice would you give to a friend who had anger outbursts over "no big deal" situations?

NO BIG DEAL: SITUATION CARDS

Someone accidentally bumps into you	Your sibling eats the last cookie
You fall and hurt yourself badly	A friend can't come over to play today
You lose a board game	Someone steals your bike
You get a question wrong on your homework	A close family member is very sick
You do poorly while playing a video game	You get lost at a store
Your favorite toy breaks and can't be fixed	A friend says something mean to you
A close friend says they don't want to be your friend anymore	Your sibling gets a bigger piece of cake than you

NO BIG DEAL: COPING CHART

- Talk to a caring adult about your feelings.

- Take deep breaths until you're calm.

- Remind yourself that upset feelings don't last forever.

- Think of something that makes you feel grateful.

- Step away from the situation to calm down.

- Imagine yourself giving advice to a friend who is going through a similar situation.

NO BIG DEAL: PRACTICE SHEET

Situation	Check One:		How I Handled It
	BIG DEAL	**NO BIG DEAL**	

SELF-CONTROL UNO*

AGES: 7+   **MODALITY:** INDIVIDUAL, GROUP, FAMILY

Introduction

The goal of this activity is to increase the ability to focus and practice self-control, particularly in relation to blurting out. By incorporating new rules into the traditional UNO game, participants will have fun while learning important self-regulation skills.

Goals

- Increase ability to focus
- Practice using self-control related to blurting out

Materials

- UNO card game

Instructions

1. Explain: "We are going to play UNO but with a few added rules to help us learn to focus!"
   - If someone lays a 7 down, everyone must stop talking until another 7 is laid down! If you talk during that time, you have to draw an extra card. If you lay down a wild card when no one is allowed to speak, you will point to the color on the card you want to pick. Likewise, if you are down to one card, instead of saying "UNO!" you will hold the card in the air.
   - If someone lays down a 6, everyone must lightly tap the table once with their thumb. The last person to tap their thumb has to draw a card.

2. Praise the client verbally or with a thumbs-up when they use self-control.

3. Ask process questions such as:
   - What did you like best about this game?
   - What was the hardest part of the game?
   - How did you feel when you had to draw an extra card?
   - How did you feel when you successfully used self-control?
   - Tell about a time when you need to stop yourself from blurting out.

---

* Intervention by Elizabeth Ernest, LMFT, LCSW

SIZE UP YOUR FEELINGS*

AGES: 7–12   **MODALITY:** INDIVIDUAL, GROUP, FAMILY

Introduction

This game not only helps children identify and express their emotions but also introduces them to coping strategies to manage those feelings effectively. By engaging in this activity, children learn to recognize the different intensities of anger and develop skills to keep their emotions under control.

Goals

- Normalize feelings of anger
- Verbally and physically express the intensity of anger
- Learn and implement helpful ways to express anger

Materials

- Expandable ball sphere (like a Hoberman sphere)
- Index cards
- Game board with a start and finish, such as Candy Land
- Tokens or game pieces (a different one for each player)
- One die

Advance Preparation

- Use the index cards to create game cards with scenarios that are age appropriate for the clients. Include a range of scenarios that might make someone feel a little angry, medium angry, or a lot angry. Make up your own or use the Anger Scenarios list on page 288.

Instructions

1. Provide age-appropriate psychoeducation about anger. This should include normalizing that everyone feels angry sometimes, noting that anger has different levels of intensity, and explaining how anger can grow and change ("get big") when we don't notice or manage it.

2. Say, "All feelings are okay to feel, even anger. But if we don't manage our anger, it can get so big that it causes other problems. When we use a helpful coping strategy to calm our anger before it gets so big, we can keep the anger small and then it's easier to deal with."

3. Hold out the expandable ball sphere in its small collapsed state: "This is what it is like when anger is small. At this point, it is easier to manage." Then expand the ball to its largest size: "This is what it is like when anger gets really big and it is harder to manage."

4. Make the ball small again: "If I am feeling just a little bit angry, I might say, 'Hmph, that makes me angry' and I might be frowning or crossing my arms." Reflect this physically and verbally.

---

* Intervention by Dina Ismailova, LCPC

5. Expand the ball to a medium size: "If I get even angrier, I might start stomping my feet and raising my voice at people around me." Reflect this physically and verbally.

6. Expand the ball to its largest size: "If my anger gets this big, I might start crying, yelling, throwing things, or hitting." Reflect this physically and verbally.

7. Ask, "What would you say/look like/do/act like if your anger is small, medium, and big?" Invite the client to use the ball sphere to show small, medium, and large, pausing at each one to give an example.

8. Emphasize how our body does different things when our anger is at a different size. Say, "Now that you know what this looks and feels like, you can notice the way anger is building up inside of you and use a coping skill to keep the anger from getting too big."

9. Teach and practice several coping skills to manage anger, such as deep breathing, tensing and relaxing muscles, and slowly counting backward from ten. (For more ideas, see the list provided on page 290).

10. Set up the game by placing the scenario cards face down in a stack beside the game board. Provide each player with a token or game piece and have them place their token at the start of the game board.

11. Explain the game: The first player draws a card from the stack and reads the scenario aloud. The player then uses the expandable sphere to show the size their feelings would be in that situation: small (a little angry or upset), medium (moderately angry or upset), or large (very angry or upset).

12. The player explains why they chose that size for their feelings. Other players can ask questions or share how they would feel.

13. After explaining their choice, the player rolls the die and moves their token forward that number of spaces on the game board.

14. Players take turns, following the same steps. The first player to reach the finish line wins!

15. Ask process questions such as:
    - Tell about a time when you felt a little angry/a lot angry.
    - What could you do if your anger starts to get too big?
    - What are some signs that your anger is starting to get bigger?

SWITCHEROO

AGES: 7–12 **MODALITY:** INDIVIDUAL, GROUP

Introduction

This activity encourages young children to think flexibly. Flexible thinking not only improves problem-solving abilities but also strengthens self-regulation. When children learn to adapt their thoughts and behaviors in response to changing situations, they develop better control over their emotions and actions, allowing them to manage frustration and setbacks more effectively.

Goals

- Develop flexible thinking skills
- Improve problem-solving skills
- Increase capacity to tolerate distress when things don't go as planned
- Improve self-regulation skills

Materials

- *Anger Scenarios* list (provided on page 288)
- Scissors
- Small, inexpensive prizes

Advance Preparation

- Photocopy the scenarios list and cut them out into individual slips of paper.

Instructions

1. Introduce the concept of flexible thinking: "Flexible thinking means being able to change your mind or plans when something doesn't go the way you expect. It's like if you wanted to play outside, but it starts raining. Instead of being upset, you can think of a new fun thing to do, like playing a game inside. Flexible thinking helps you come up with different ideas and keeps you calm when things don't go your way or when plans change."

2. Teach the three-step flexible thinking strategy:
   - Take three deep breaths.
   - Say to yourself, "I'm upset that things didn't go my way, but I can think of another plan or idea."
   - Come up with an appropriate new plan or idea.

3. Explain that you will pick one of the scenario paper slips and put it behind your back. The client guesses which hand the paper is in. If they guess correctly, they receive two points. If they guess incorrectly, they receive one point.

4. The client then reads the scenario and demonstrates the three-step flexible thinking strategy they would use to cope with it.

5. You can also use the game itself as an opportunity for the client to use the strategy in real time, such as when they guess the wrong hand.

6. At the end, clients trade in points for prizes: 1–12 points = 1 prize, and 13 or more points = 2 prizes.

7. Ask process questions such as:

   - What was your favorite scenario?
   - Tell about a time when plans suddenly changed, how you felt, and what you did about it.
   - How can this strategy help you when you don't get what you want or when things don't go as planned?

THUMBS-UP, THUMBS-DOWN

Introduction

This game is designed to increase sustained attention and improve impulse control through a series of commands where children must respond correctly based on visual cues.

Goals

- Increase sustained attention
- Improve impulse control

Instructions

1. Explain: "I will say a command and then give a thumbs-up or a thumbs-down. If I give a thumbs-up, follow the command. If I give a thumbs-down, do not follow the command. You earn one point for each correct move. Let's see how many points you can get!"

2. Give the client a series of commands, randomly accompanied by either a thumbs-up or a thumbs-down. Examples include:

   - Look up
   - Sit down
   - Touch your nose
   - Hop on your left foot three times
   - Jump up once
   - Clap three times
   - Hop on your right foot three times
   - Look down
   - Tap your knees two times
   - Touch your nose

   - Tap your head four times
   - Spin around once
   - Touch your toes
   - Stand on one foot
   - Wave your hand
   - Pat your shoulders
   - Wiggle your fingers
   - Stomp your feet twice
   - Close your eyes
   - Touch your ears

3. Ask process questions such as:

   - Was it easy or hard to stop yourself from following the command when I gave a thumbs-down?
   - Give an example of when you have to follow a command at home or at school.
   - What does impulse control mean? Give an example of when you have to have good impulse control at home or at school.

NO FAIR!

AGES: 5–10	**MODALITY:** INDIVIDUAL, GROUP, FAMILY

Introduction

This intervention provides children with an opportunity to learn to tolerate jealousy and unfairness using the game format as an engaging tool. It helps them develop emotional regulation by recognizing that unfair situations are a part of life. Children will practice strategies for managing their feelings in a safe and supportive environment, which can enhance their social relationships and overall emotional well-being. Through gameplay, children will learn that while unfairness can feel upsetting, they have the power to respond calmly and appropriately.

Goals

- Normalize feelings of jealousy, anger, and disappointment when faced with situations that are perceived as unfair
- Increase capacity to tolerate jealousy and unfairness
- Strengthen emotional regulation when dealing with upsetting feelings
- Encourage problem-solving skills and flexible thinking

Materials

- *No Fair! Scenarios* template (provided)
- 16 envelopes
- Scissors
- Two small non-food prizes
- Puppets or dolls (optional)

Advance Preparation

- Photocopy the scenarios, cut them out, and place one scenario in each envelope. Place the envelopes on a table or on the floor, spread out.

Instructions

1. Provide psychoeducation on the relationship between jealousy, anger, and fairness: "Jealousy is a feeling that happens when someone has something that you want. It could be an object, a skill, or even attention from adults. When someone else gets what we want, we might think it's 'no fair.' Feeling jealous or thinking that something is unfair can make you feel angry or upset, which may lead to making poor choices that might get you in trouble."

2. Discuss inappropriate ways to handle unfairness, such as crying, yelling, running away, putting your hands on someone, cheating, or sulking.

3. Then discuss appropriate ways to handle unfairness, such as taking a deep breath, focusing on the good things you have, or using helpful self-talk (e.g., "It doesn't always have to be

equal," "It's no big deal," "Win some, lose some," "I'll get a chance another time," "I don't like what happened, but I choose to stay calm").

4. Explain: "This game will help you learn appropriate ways to handle situations that you think are no fair."

5. Have the players take turns choosing an envelope and opening it. If the player picks an envelope with a scenario, they read it out loud. Then that player performs two skits in response to the scenario: one that demonstrates an inappropriate way to handle the unfair scenario, and one demonstrating an appropriate way to handle it. (Optional: Have the players use puppets or dolls to act out the scenarios.)

6. If a player picks an envelope that reads "PRIZE!" they get a small prize. The other players have to say to themselves, "I'm upset I didn't get a prize, but I choose to stay calm."

7. The game continues until all the envelopes are empty.

8. Ask process questions such as:
   - How might other kids feel if they see you get very angry when you think that something unfair happened?
   - Tell about a time when something happened that you felt was unfair, and you got very upset. How did you handle it?
   - Can you think of a situation when you stayed calm even though something seemed unfair? How did it make you feel?
   - What are some other ways to help yourself feel better when things seem unfair?
   - Why do you think it's important to stay calm when something is unfair, even if you don't like it?

Variation

- **Fairness Role-Reversal:** After a scenario is read, ask the child to imagine how the other person in the situation might feel (e.g., how the sibling with the bigger piece of cake might feel). This encourages empathy and helps children see situations from multiple perspectives.

NO FAIR! SCENARIOS

Your sibling gets a bigger piece of cake than you.	Your sibling gets to stay up later than you.
You are sitting with your friend at school at lunch time and you notice that they got a better snack than you.	You have a cold, so you have to stay home while everyone else in your family gets to go to the carnival.
You're playing a board game with your friend and they keep winning.	You get into a fight with someone in your class at school. You get into trouble but your classmate does not get into trouble.
Your team keeps losing.	Your sibling got a new pair of shoes but you didn't.
Your friend got a video game that you really want.	Your sibling gets to sit beside your parent.
Your sibling gets to pick the show or movie to watch.	You keep raising your hand in class but your teacher keeps picking other kidsw.
Someone else got the part that you wanted in the play.	You have to have a bath instead of staying outside to play with your friends.
PRIZE!	PRIZE!

CHAPTER 4:

Social Skills

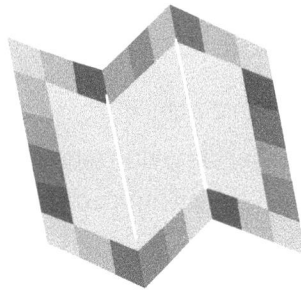

Many children lack basic social skills and as a result, they are often alienated from their peers. Learning to relate appropriately to others is, therefore, an important treatment goal for many clients. As would be expected, socialization activities are most appropriate for use in group counseling settings so children can learn, practice, and rehearse prosocial behaviors. The therapist can observe the group dynamics and provide constructive feedback to children on how they relate to others. Children can also gain insight into their behavior by accepting feedback from their peers.

Since games are designed to be engaging, they are an ideal tool to motivate clients to work on social skills. The rules and objectives of the game provide an appropriate context to reinforce skill acquisition and to help clients build social competence. Games create a safe space where children can experiment with social interactions, and the fun nature of games makes them less threatening than traditional social skills training. Furthermore, games encourage children to step outside their comfort zones and engage with peers in new ways, fostering empathy and understanding.

As children practice these social skills, they learn not only to interact more effectively with others but also to recognize and regulate their own emotions in social contexts. The repetition and structure games offer enable children to develop these skills gradually and naturally, promoting long-term social growth.

The games in this chapter can be incorporated into a social skills curriculum to help children master a variety of social behaviors.

BUBBLES

Introduction

This game facilitates prosocial behavior by providing an environment for children to rehearse social skills and gain immediate peer feedback. The combination of group play and process questions enables children to integrate the skills.

Goals

- Acquire awareness of socially acceptable behavior
- Practice and improve appropriate social behaviors such as following rules, turn-taking, sharing, being polite, making eye contact, giving compliments, personal space, fairness, and self-control

Materials

- Bubbles

Instructions

1. Explain: "These bubbles are going to be passed around the group. Each of you will have a turn to blow bubbles three times as long as you follow the rules." There are five rules:

   - Calmly and patiently wait your turn.
   - Share the bubbles by passing them to the next person when your turn is over.
   - When it is your turn, make eye contact with the person holding the bubbles and say, "Please may I play with the bubbles?"
   - When the person gives you the bubbles, make eye contact with them and say, "Thank you for giving me the bubbles."
   - When it is your turn, you get three blows, regardless of how many bubbles come out of the bubble wand.

2. Then explain: "If you break any of these rules, you miss your turn. Let's see if we can all play the game by following the rules." Before commencing the activity, give the players a verbal quiz about the rules to make sure they understand the expectations.

3. Have the players stand in a circle and proceed with the game. Have them pass the bubbles around the circle twice. (You may wish to hold the bubble jar while the children dip the wand to avoid spills.)

4. As the children play, remind them of the five rules and praise them by making comments such as, "I like how you are waiting patiently for your turn," "It's nice to hear you say please and thank you," and "You know how to share."

5. Depending on the age of the group members, additional rounds can be played with more advanced skills:

- **Giving compliments and appropriate winning and losing reactions:** Two group members compete to see how many bubbles they can blow. The player watching the bubble blower must give a compliment, such as "You did a good job blowing a lot of bubbles." The loser (the player who blew the fewer amount of bubbles) must make eye contact with the winner and politely say, "Good game."

- **Fairness:** Give one group member an extra turn, then discuss ways to handle a situation where someone gets more.

- **Respect personal space:** Discuss personal space. Members must stand four feet apart and blow bubbles away from others.

- **Invite others to play:** Give the bubbles to one member, who must then invite another member to play with them by asking, "Would you like to blow bubbles with me?"

6. Ask process questions such as:

- Say one thing we practiced today.

- Was it easy or hard to patiently wait your turn?

- Tell about other times when you must patiently wait your turn, share, and say please and thank you.

CANDY LAND: SOCIAL SKILLS VERSION*

Introduction

This version of Candy Land encourages children to practice important social behaviors such as turn-taking, making eye contact, and listening to others. Through role-playing and questions, children will explore positive interactions with peers, learn how to handle winning and losing, and develop cooperation skills in a supportive environment.

Goals

- Practice and improve appropriate social behaviors such as following rules, turn-taking, eye contact, and listening
- Increase ability to appropriately tolerate losing a game

Materials

- Candy Land board game
- *Candy Land: Social Skills Version Prompts* (provided)

Advance Preparation

- Before the session, prepare a list of questions tailored to the needs of the client(s). Alternatively, you can use the prompts provided.

Instructions

1. Set up the Candy Land board as usual.

2. Players take turns picking a card from the deck. If the color on the card is different from their pawn's square or if they pick a picture card, they must answer a social skills question before moving to the appropriate square on the game board. If the card's color matches their pawn's square, they move immediately to that color and get an extra turn without answering a question.

3. Alternate version: Whenever the players land on a square that is the same color as their pawn, they must answer a question.

4. Throughout the game, encourage and praise players for making good eye contact and using polite words. You can create more opportunities for this by modifying the game rules (e.g., if a player draws a card of a specific color, they cannot touch their own pawn that turn and must politely ask another player to move it for them).

5. Ask process questions such as:
   - Say something you learned from this game.
   - What was it like to practice making eye contact and using polite words?
   - What will you do next time you play a game and someone else wins?

---

* Intervention by Gary G. F. Yorke, PhD

CANDY LAND: SOCIAL SKILLS VERSION PROMPTS

- How would you feel if somebody did not follow the rules of the game?

- Say one important rule of this game that must be followed by all the players.

- In this game, we have to take turns. What's another game you like to play that involves taking turns?

- What are some words you can use when you want to play with someone?

- When is it a good idea to take turns?

- Ask another player to tell you about their favorite meal. Listen carefully, and then tell them what they said.

- Pretend you're talking to a new student in your class. What would you say first? What are some other polite and friendly things you can say or ask?

- What is a nice way to ask somebody to play with you?

- Your friend comes to your house to play. Being a good friend means letting them decide what to play. What words can you use so they get to decide what to play?

- What are some words you can use when you are leaving your friend's house after a playdate?

- Ask another person to stare at your nose. Does it look like they are making eye contact? Show what eye contact looks like.

- Someone in your class falls down while running in the schoolyard. What would be a nice thing to say to them?

- Grab another player's piece. Now give it back and say, "I'm sorry, I won't do that again."

- What can you say to someone when they win a game?

- What can you say to yourself when you lose a game?

COOTIE*

Introduction

This activity uses the classic Cootie game to help young children develop important social skills such as following rules, turn-taking, making eye contact, and listening. By associating each part of the cootie with a specific behavior, children practice positive interactions and learn how to appropriately tolerate losing a game.

Goals

- Practice and improve appropriate social behaviors such as following rules, turn-taking, eye contact, and listening
- Increase ability to appropriately tolerate losing a game

Materials

- Cootie board game
- One standard die

Instructions

1. Each player rolls the die. The player with the highest roll starts the game.

2. Each player will be constructing their own cootie. One body, one head, two antennae, two eyes, one proboscis, and six legs are required to make a complete cootie. Each part of the cootie's body is identified by a number: 1 = body, 2 = head, 3 = antennae, 4 = eyes, 5 = proboscis, and 6 = legs.

3. First, each player tries to get the body of the cootie by rolling a 1 on the die. If the player succeeds, they get a free roll to try for the head. The body must be obtained first, then the head, before any other parts of the cootie can be attached. The antennae, eyes, proboscis, and legs can be acquired in any order once the body and head have been acquired.

4. The player loses the die if they fail to roll the number for an eligible part that they have not yet acquired, but they get a free roll if they succeed. For example, if the player rolls a 4 and already has the eyes, then the die gets passed to the next player. If they roll a 4 and don't yet have the eyes, they pick them up and roll again.

5. Each body part also corresponds with a social skill as follows:
   - When 1 is rolled and the body is acquired, instruct the player to say: "Cootie wants to play."
   - When 2 is rolled and the head is acquired, have the player say: "Cootie is going to use their brain to remember and follow the rules of the game."

---
* Intervention by Gary G. F. Yorke, PhD

- When 3 is rolled and the antenna is acquired, have the player say: "Cootie is going to listen carefully when somebody is talking."
- When 4 is rolled and the eyes are acquired, have the player say: "Cootie is going to look at the person they are talking to."
- When 5 is rolled and the proboscis is acquired, have the player say: "Cootie is going to keep their hands and feet to themselves when they play."
- When 6 is rolled and the legs are acquired, instruct the player to walk their cootie to the next player, gently hand them the die, and say: "It's your turn now."

6. When a player has acquired all the body parts and their cootie is complete, they are the winner. The other players say to the winner: "Good game!"

7. Ask process questions such as:
   - How did you feel when you had to wait for your turn?
   - What do you think helped you follow the rules of the game?
   - How did it feel to say "Good game" to the winner? Why is that important?
   - What was hard about making sure Cootie listened carefully or looked at the person talking?

8. This game can be used to develop many other skills, such as frustration tolerance, impulse control, talking about feelings, listening the first time, and cooperating and sharing.

DICE GAME*

Introduction

This dice game encourages participants to articulate feelings, practice prosocial behaviors like empathy and assertiveness, and apply appropriate coping techniques when facing challenging emotions.

Goals

- Verbally articulate a range of emotions
- Practice and improve appropriate social behaviors such as empathy, communication, and assertiveness
- Learn, practice, and implement an appropriate self-calming strategy when feeling upset (e.g., anxious, angry, sad, scared)

Materials

- *Coping Cards*, *Feeling Cards*, and *Social Scenario Cards* (provided)
- Three sheets of paper in different colors or coloring utensils
- Scissors
- One die

Advance Preparation

- Print and cut out the game cards. Use different colored paper or mark the backs of the cards in some way to differentiate between the three types of cards.

Instructions

1. Explain: "This game will help us talk about feelings, discuss ways to handle social situations, and practice coping strategies."

2. The person whose birthday was most recent will go first. They will roll the dice and choose the card that corresponds with the number they rolled:

   - **1 or 4 = Coping Card:** Everyone will practice the technique together.
   - **2 or 5 = Feeling Card:** Talk about a time you felt that feeling.
   - **3 or 6 = Social Scenario Card:** Discuss what you would do in that situation.

3. Ask process questions such as:

   - Of the feelings drawn, which was the hardest/easiest for you to talk about?
   - Discuss one of the social situations and how you would feel if it happened to you.
   - Name your favorite self-calming technique that we practiced during the game.

---

* Intervention by Erika Walker, LSCSW, LCSW, LICSW, RPT-S™

DICE GAME: COPING CARDS

Breathe: Take a deep breath in through your nose (like smelling a flower) then blow it out gently through your mouth (like blowing out a candle).

Robot, Ragdoll: Tighten your body like a stiff robot, then make your body go floppy like a ragdoll.

Butterfly Hug: Cross your arms over your chest and gently tap one hand on your shoulder, then the other, like butterfly wings flapping.

Music: Make a calming playlist and listen to it when you need to feel calm. Name a few songs you'd like on your playlist.

Talk: Talk to someone about how you're feeling—it really does help! Who is someone you could talk to?

Calm Place: Create a place in your imagination that you can go to when you need to feel calm. Describe one part of it.

Rainbow Noticing: Look around and say three things you see that correspond with three colors of a rainbow.

Lemon Squeeze: Imagine you're holding a lemon in your hands and squeezing it to make lemonade. Hold for a few seconds and then release.

Proud Moment: Thinking of a proud moment can help you feel better. Tell about a proud moment now.

Calm Thoughts: Thinking calm thoughts is a helpful way to feel better. Give an example of a calm thought.

DICE GAME: FEELING CARDS

Excited	**Angry**
Nervous	**Excluded**
Frustrated	**Brave**
Jealous	**Sad**
Scared	**Proud**

DICE GAME: SOCIAL SCENARIO CARDS

Your friend is standing off by themselves and when you approach them, you see they have tears in their eyes.

The teacher assigns you to do a group project with a kid who has bullied you in the past.

Your aunt gives you a gift that you don't like.

You are in the lunchroom and another student bullies you when the teachers aren't looking.

You're playing a game with your friend and they start to cheat.

You see a group of children playing soccer at recess and you want to join the game.

You're at recess and your friend wants to play soccer, but you want to play hide and seek.

One of your friends tells you that someone said something hurtful about you.

You are having a difficult time understanding something in class, and you feel shy about asking a question out loud.

Your friend has just arrived at your home for a playdate.

FRIENDLY CHALLENGE

AGES: 9+   **MODALITY:** GROUP

Introduction

This intervention uses the board game *Beat That!* This modified version promotes turn-taking, problem-solving, and communication while fostering an atmosphere of encouragement and cooperation among players.

Goals

- Practice and improve appropriate social behaviors such as turn-taking, positive encouragement, and communication
- Strengthen group cooperation and cohesion

Materials

- Beat That! board game (includes 160 challenge cards, 80 betting tokens, 10 cups, 5 dice, 4 balls, measuring tape, and a sand timer)

Advance Preparation

- Read through the challenge cards and select 10 that are most appropriate to the group members. They should be engaging and not overly challenging.

Instructions

1. Set up the game as follows: Distribute 10 betting tokens to each player (5 blue, 3 orange, 2 yellow). Set aside the remaining tokens to be distributed for bonus points. Have all other game items ready for use. Place the 10 preselected challenge cards in the center of the playing area.

2. Players take turns picking the top challenge card from the deck. Each card will explain the challenge and what equipment is needed. There are four challenge categories:

   - **Solo Challenges:** These are challenges that one player completes on their own.
   - **Battle Royale:** All players compete at the same time, and the winner is awarded points.
   - **Buddy-Up:** Players pair up to complete challenges.
   - **Head-to-Head:** Two players compete directly.

3. Before attempting the challenge, each player must bet one of their tokens based on how confident they are in their (or their team's) ability to complete the challenge. Tokens are colored according to their value (blue = 1 point, orange = 3 points, yellow = 5 points). Only one token can be bet by each player per challenge. Once a token has been bet, it cannot be used again.

4. If the player succeeds in the challenge, they win points equal to the value of the token they bet. If they fail, they do not receive any points.

5. In case of a tie at the end of the challenge, the tied players can do a final "sudden death" challenge to determine the winner.

6. In this adapted version of the game, players can earn one bonus point per round as follows:
   - **After a Solo Challenge:** If that player successfully completes the task, all other players must congratulate them. If the player is unsuccessful, all other players say in an encouraging tone, "You tried your best."
   - **After a Battle Royale:** All players must congratulate the winner.
   - **After a Buddy-Up:** If they successfully completed the task together, they give each other a gentle high five. If they were unsuccessful, they shake hands and say, "We tried our best."
   - **After a Head-to-Head:** The winner says to their opponent, "Good job!"

7. Additional bonus points are also awarded when players demonstrate prosocial behavior (e.g., waiting patiently for their turn, following the rules of the game, cooperating with their teammate).

8. After 10 rounds, the player with the most points wins the game. All players shake hands at the end.

9. Ask process questions such as:
   - How did it feel to encourage others after their challenges, whether they succeeded or not?
   - What was it like to wait patiently for your turn? Tell about a time at school or at home when you must wait patiently for your turn.
   - What was the most difficult challenge for you, and how did you handle it?
   - How did your feelings change when working with a partner versus competing individually?
   - What strategies did you and your teammates use to support each other during the game?

I'M SORRY!*

Introduction

This intervention builds upon the classic Sorry! board game to help children and adolescents better understand the complexities of apologies. While many children are taught to say "sorry" after negative behaviors, they may not fully grasp the significance of the apology or why it's important. A simple "sorry" can sometimes feel hollow, failing to repair the relationship or convey genuine remorse. This game aims to bridge that gap by encouraging players to reflect on apologies and practice more meaningful, empathetic expressions of remorse. Participants will improve their social skills, gain a deeper understanding of taking responsibility, and practice showing empathy when apologies are needed. The experience is designed to be engaging and interactive, allowing clients to explore the concept of apologies in a safe and supportive environment.

Goals

- Improve social skills by practicing ways to verbalize and mean an apology
- Encourage taking responsibility when an apology is needed
- Increase empathy

Materials

- Sorry! board game
- *Apology Scenario Cards* (provided)
- Cardstock
- Scissors

Advance Preparation

- Photocopy the *Apology Scenario Cards* onto cardstock (or create your own scenarios) and cut them into individual cards.

Instructions

1. Explain: "Today we are going to play the game 'I'm Sorry!' where we will use the Sorry! board game to learn and practice making apologies. We will follow the usual board game instructions, except that when a player draws a Sorry card, they also draw a scenario card and provide a response out loud before moving another player's pawn back to start."

2. When playing with a family, encourage them to respond to the apology scenarios using examples that happened in real life between the members who are playing.

---

* Intervention by Jamie Lynn Langley, LCSW, RPT-S™. Adapted with permission from "Utilizing Games to Build Resilience in Children Impacted by Divorce," by J. L. Langley, in J. Stone, & C. E. Schaefer, (Eds.) *Game Play Therapy: Therapeutic Use of Games with Children and Adolescents* (3rd ed.), 2020, John Wiley & Sons.

3. Ask process questions such as:
    - What makes an apology feel genuine to you? How can we make sure the other person knows we mean it when we say sorry?
    - Think about a time when someone apologized to you. How did you feel about this? What could have made that apology better?
    - Why is it important to include empathy in an apology? Think of a situation where showing empathy while apologizing could make a difference.

APOLOGY SCENARIO CARDS

Think about a time someone said "Sorry!" but it did not seem like they meant it. Briefly describe that situation and how you felt about it. What do you wish they had said instead?

Tell about a time you felt sorry for something you did but did not know how to say sorry. How could you apologize now? Consider if there is a way to still say it to the person involved.

Has there been a time when you wanted someone to apologize to you for something that happened, but they did not? How did that feel? What do you wish they would have said when they apologized?

Has there been a time a parent or other adult apologized to you? What was that like? Did it feel genuine? If so, how did they express their apology? If not, what could they have said instead?

Think of a time when an adult instructed you to make an apology. Describe that situation and what you apologized for. Then practice saying that apology, including what you did and why you are sorry.

Has there been a time that you apologized because you were instructed to by an adult, but you did not feel you had anything to apologize for? How did that feel? How would you state that apology now? Or, if you would not apologize now, what would you say instead?

What does it mean to be empathetic to another person? How can a well-intentioned apology be empathetic? State an example of an empathetic apology.

Think about a situation when someone apologized to you, but you didn't feel ready to forgive them. How did it feel to hear their apology? Is there anything they could have done or said differently that might have helped you feel better?

Describe a situation where you had to apologize to multiple people for something you did. How did you feel? What did you say? Reimagine that apology and practice delivering it with empathy to the group.

Reflect on a time someone apologized to you, but you felt it wasn't necessary because no harm was done. How did you react? Discuss why sometimes people say "sorry" out of habit.

LEGO TOWER POWER

Introduction

This game is designed to promote appropriate social behaviors such as turn-taking, problem-solving, and communication. By engaging in a cooperative activity that requires teamwork to build the tallest LEGO tower, the game helps strengthen group cohesion and fosters a supportive and collaborative environment.

Goals

- Practice and improve appropriate social behavior such as turn-taking, problem-solving, and communication
- Strengthen group cooperation and cohesion

Materials

- LEGO
- Timer

Instructions

1. Divide the group into two teams and instruct each team to sit in a circle. Divide the LEGO pieces evenly among the teams and place them in the center of each circle.

2. Explain that the teams have two minutes to build the tallest tower possible with their LEGO pieces. They must follow these rules:

    - The team member whose first name is closest to the letter A goes first, and then the rest go clockwise.
    - Team members take turns adding one block to the tower at a time until the two-minute timer goes off.
    - The towers are measured by how many blocks high they are, earning one point per block of height. Two bonus points are awarded if the tower follows a pattern (e.g., rows in alternating colors).
    - The teams can also earn bonus points for group cooperation, turn-taking, positive encouragement, and appropriate enthusiasm, which you will award as you observe their teamwork.

3. Ask process questions such as:

    - How did each person feel during the building process?
    - What kind of atmosphere was created in the group (cooperative or uncooperative)?
    - Give examples of positive encouragement, and how it felt.
    - What did you learn today about working together?

LIE TO ME*

Introduction

This engaging activity aims to help participants understand the implications of lying and to reduce the frequency of lying. It explores the reasons behind lying through interactive and reflective exercises.

Goals

- Understand the act of lying and its implications
- Decrease the act of lying

Materials

- Index cards
- Writing utensils
- Whiteboard or large sheet of paper taped to the wall

Instructions

1. Divide the players into pairs.

2. Distribute two cards to each player for each round. On one card, players write a truth and on the other a lie about themselves or about a situation that has happened to them.

3. Each player in the pair takes a turn reading their two cards (a truth and a lie) aloud, trying to convince the other player that both are true. The objective of the game is to narrate the lie in a credible way to try to deceive the opponent.

4. The opponent must guess which of the two is the lie. If the player who reads the cards manages to fool their opponent, they win a point. If the opponent correctly guesses the lie, they win the point.

5. The points are recorded on a board or a sheet of paper. After five rounds, the player in each pair with the most points wins.

6. Ask process questions such as:
   - Why might somebody lie? (If the clients are unable to identify reasons, then offer examples such as fear, avoiding consequences, or wanting to impress others).
   - How do you feel when someone lies to you? Why do you think you feel that way?
   - What might be some consequences of lying, even if it seems harmless at the moment?
   - Tell about a time you lied. Why did you lie?
   - What advice would you give to someone who felt they should lie in order to impress others?
   - What are some good reasons to be honest?

---

* Intervention by Arlen Sarabia, PhD

NO RULES PICK-UP STICKS*

Introduction

This game emphasizes the importance of rules and fair play, teaching this concept in a playful and engaging manner. Initially, the child is taken aback when the therapist declares an unfair victory without adhering to any rules, but they quickly understand that the exercise is designed to highlight the necessity of all players following the same rules.

Goals

- Increase understanding of the importance of rules during gameplay
- Practice and improve appropriate social behavior such as following rules and turn-taking
- Increase the ability to appropriately tolerate losing a game

Materials

- Pick-up sticks

Instructions

1. Explain to the client that you are going to play "No Rules Pick-Up Sticks." Drop the sticks on the floor, quickly pick them all up, and announce in an enthusiastic tone, "I won!" The child will likely respond by saying something like, "No fair!" Reply that it *was* fair, since the game had no rules. Ask the client if they enjoyed the game. (Their answer, of course, will be "no.") This leads to a discussion about the need for rules and playing fair when taking part in a game with someone.

2. Together with the client, brainstorm a list of rules to follow while playing pick-up sticks.

3. Play again, but this time, both players must follow the rules. Model and verbalize appropriate rule-following behavior, such as: "I'm going to concentrate and go slow so I have a better chance of getting more sticks" and "I really wanted to pretend that this stick didn't move, but I'm going to follow the rules so it's fair for both of us."

4. Ask process questions such as:
   - Why is it important for all players to follow the rules?
   - What could you do if you feel like cheating in order to win a game?
   - Would you want to play with someone who cheats?
   - What would be an appropriate way to handle another player cheating?
   - What would be an appropriate way to handle losing a game?

---

* Intervention by Scott Riviere, MS, LPC, LMFT, RPT-S™

ONE WORD*

Introduction

This activity aims to enhance social skills by encouraging participants to engage in conversation, make and maintain eye contact, and practice listening and turn-taking.

Goals

- Practice and improve appropriate social behaviors such as making and maintaining eye contact, initiating and having an appropriate conversation, listening, and turn-taking
- Increase comfort in talking

Materials

- Index cards and writing utensil
- Timer
- Small, inexpensive prizes

Instructions

1. Explain that the object of this game is to practice getting comfortable initiating and maintaining an appropriate conversation with another person.

2. Have the players brainstorm a list of at least 10 topic words. These can be objects, feelings, names, foods, places, school subjects, colors, TV shows, animals, or even the weather. Write each word on a separate index card and shuffle the cards.

3. Divide the players into pairs and give each pair a few game cards, face down. Assign one person or pair as the group's timekeeper for each round (or you can be the timekeeper throughout). In each pair, player A is the person whose first name comes first alphabetically; the other is player B.

4. Player A picks the top card from the pile of game cards. The timekeeper sets the timer for 15 seconds and calls out, "Start talking!" Player A must talk to player B about the topic word for the duration. Player A must use the topic word at least once and use coherent, related, flowing sentences.

5. When the time is up, the timekeeper has everyone stop and resets the timer for another 15 seconds. Player B then expands on anything player A said about the given word for that time. After this, players A and B will switch roles and do the exercise again with a new topic card.

6. If needed, provide an example of inappropriate and appropriate conversation before beginning the gameplay. For instance, an inappropriate way to talk about the topic word "book" might be: "Book. I like books. I went swimming. I want to go outside. Is my turn over yet?" An

---

* Intervention by Norma Leben, LCSW-S, ACSW, RPT-S™ (retired)

appropriate way might be: "Book. I like books, especially picture books about the zoo. I think the animals are beautiful, especially the tigers. The elephants are so big, too. I like to go to the library and find books about animals."

7. After the first round of 15-second conversations, consider subsequent rounds with increased lengths of time (30 seconds, one minute).

8. Players earn one point for each round in which they maintain an appropriate conversation for the given amount of time, and one point for using the topic word at least once. Consider additional points for using appropriate eye contact. Points are determined by the player's partner. Emphasize that they must *not* judge based on whether they found the conversation interesting, funny, awkward, and so on; the goal is simply to practice engaging with others and staying on topic. With more practice at longer duration, encourage personal sharing (e.g., ideas, dreams, plans, or feelings stimulated by the word).

9. At the end, award small prizes to all players.

10. Ask process questions such as:
    - How did it feel to talk for a set amount of time about a word? Was it difficult or easy?
    - What strategies did you use to keep the conversation going?
    - How did you feel when your partner expanded on your word? Did anything they say surprise you?
    - What did you learn about starting and maintaining conversations from this activity? How can you use this in real life?

TIME, PLACE, AND PEOPLE CHITCHAT*

AGES: 10+	**MODALITY:** GROUP

Introduction

This game aims to enhance communication skills by encouraging players to understand the importance of turn-taking, active listening, and adapting their communication style based on the context and the person they are speaking with. It provides an interactive way to practice these skills, teaching players how to recognize social cues and respond appropriately in diverse situations. The goal is for participants to communicate respectfully and clearly, even in unfamiliar or challenging circumstances, preparing them for real-life social interactions.

Goals

- Practice and improve communication skills such as initiating and having an appropriate conversation
- Develop the ability to adapt communication styles based on different contexts and roles
- Encourage teamwork and collaboration through cooperative role-playing scenarios

Materials

- Three envelopes
- Index cards in two different colors
- Name tag labels
- Markers

Advance Preparation

- Label the three envelopes: "TIME," "PLACE," and "PEOPLE."

Instructions

1. Give each player three cards of each color and three name labels.

2. Ask the players to write a specific time on each of their cards of the first color (e.g., New Year's Eve at midnight, the first day of summer vacation, the day after a tornado). Put these cards into the envelope marked TIME.

3. Next, ask the players to write a specific place on each of the second set of cards (e.g., the school gym, a deserted island, the cereal aisle at the grocery store). Put these cards into the PLACE envelope.

4. Finally, ask the players to write roles of people on the name labels (e.g., grandparent, movie star, dog groomer). Place these in the PEOPLE envelope.

5. Explain: "This game will help you practice having conversations. For an appropriate conversation, it is important for people to take turns speaking and listening. In addition, it is important to keep in mind the time of the conversation, the location, and to whom you are talking."

---

* Intervention by Norma Leben, LCSW-S, ACSW, RPT-S™ (retired)

6. Explain how the game works: You will pick a card from the TIME envelope and a card from the PLACE envelope. Each player will pick a name tag from the PEOPLE envelope, stick it on their shirt, and pretend to be that person in a role-play conversation centered around the chosen time and place.

7. If needed, provide an example, such as: "One rainy day in May (time card) on a deserted island (place card), a doctor (people card) says, 'Oh no, our sailboat was wrecked in the storm and we're stuck here. Do you, fisher (another player's people card), know how to fish these waters so we can eat?' The fisher says, 'I do. Maybe this songwriter (another player's people card) can help me?' The songwriter answers, 'I'm not hungry. I feel a song coming; I need to go write it down. Bye!' The fisher snaps back, 'Who died and made you boss?'"

8. After the role-play interaction, the players should stop, briefly evaluate the situation, and offer feedback to one another. You can then begin a new round with a different scenario.

9. Ask process questions such as:
   - What was challenging about maintaining the conversation in your assigned role?
   - How did you feel when someone responded unexpectedly to your character?
   - What strategies can you use to ensure everyone gets a chance to speak in a conversation?

TUMBLING LIES*

AGES: 8+   **MODALITY:** INDIVIDUAL, GROUP, FAMILY

Introduction

This game is designed for children to explore lying. This game helps build an understanding of how lying can impact relationships with peers, at school, or within a family and how it can make life more challenging. The game uses visual elements to illustrate how lies can become more complex over time.

Goals

- Identify the impact of lies over time
- Increase insight into the consequences of lying
- Develop an understanding of how lying impacts relationships

Materials

- Block stacking game (such as Jenga)

Instructions

1. Explain that you'll be playing a version of Jenga that will help them understand and explore lying. Play the traditional way, but as each block is removed, the player must share a reason people lie or something people may lie about. These statements can be personal or general/hypothetical.

2. Observe how the game itself serves as a metaphor about how lies can become more complex over time. As the game progresses, the lies make it more challenging to maintain a balance. In the end, there will be no more easy moves, and the final "lie" will cause the tower to fall.

3. During gameplay, ask process questions such as:
   - What does it mean to tell a lie?
   - What are some reasons people lie?
   - How are people feeling before they lie?
   - How might someone feel after lying?
   - Do you think lying makes the problem bigger or smaller?
   - Why might someone be afraid to tell the truth?

4. After the game, ask further process questions such as:
   - How do you feel when someone lies to you?
   - How is the tumbling tower like lying?
   - How does lying affect the person who is lying?
   - How does telling a lie lead to telling more lies and make a small problem bigger?

---

* Intervention by Lisa Remey MEd, LPC-S, RPT-S™, NCC

- What do you think lying does to trust in a relationship?
- What good things can happen when someone chooses to be honest? How would they feel?

Note: Remember that it is common for children to tell lies, and there are several factors that contribute to this behavior, like the child's stage of development. For example, a young child may lie to express a wish or a fantasy. An older child may lie to avoid getting into trouble, for personal gain, or to help someone else feel better. Be sure to normalize the client's experiences with lying without endorsing dishonesty.

UNO EXTREME*

Introduction

This is an interactive game designed to enhance communication, foster cohesion, and practice patience and turn-taking. By adding creative "extreme" rules, participants not only enjoy the game but also practice implementing appropriate coping skills. This game also encourages players to think flexibly as they adapt to new and unexpected rules, which helps them become more comfortable with changes and challenges in a playful setting.

Goals

- Strengthen group/family cohesion and communication
- Practice and improve appropriate social behaviors, such as following game rules, turn-taking, and having patience
- Practice and implement appropriate coping skills and flexible thinking

Materials

- UNO card game
- Whiteboard or large sheet of paper taped to the wall and writing utensil

Instructions

1. "UNO Extreme" is played like regular UNO with an extremely wild twist: Each player sets one rule that is enforced for all players when a number card of their choice is played and will continue to be enforced until that number is played again. The exception is if the stated rule is a one-time rule such as swapping or passing hands.

2. Share with the players the extreme rule options:
   - Play the game in silence
   - Play the game in a whisper voice
   - Swap hands with anyone
   - Don't show your teeth
   - Everyone slaps the deck when this card is played; last one to slap draws a card
   - Add a card to anyone's deck from the draw pile
   - Give a card away out of your deck

3. Ask all participants for their chosen number and rule and write these on a whiteboard, large sheet of paper, or similar to help them remember.

4. Play regular UNO, beginning with seven cards. If a card is played that does not have an extreme rule, no action is needed. If a card is played with an extreme rule, the players must

---

* Intervention by Kelly Pullen MA, LPC-S, RPT™

follow that rule until the next card of the same number is played. Each time a player forgets to follow an extreme rule that is in effect, they must draw a card.

5. Ask process questions such as:

- Which extreme rule was your favorite?
- Which extreme rule was the most difficult to follow?
- What was challenging about following the rules, and how did you manage those challenges?
- How did you cope when you or someone else made a mistake or forgot a rule?
- How can the patience and communication skills practiced in the game help you in other situations?

WHO, WHAT, WHERE, AND WHEN*

AGES: 7–16   **MODALITY:** INDIVIDUAL, GROUP

Introduction

Young clients struggling with highly sensitive stressors and presenting problems—such as sexual abuse, parental incarceration, substance abuse, contentious divorces, or sensitive health conditions—may need assistance discriminating between appropriate situations to discuss these matters outside of session and times in which it might be in the client's best interest to protect their privacy. This intervention is designed to help the client strengthen interpersonal boundaries in regard to discussing a sensitive issue or event with individuals in a position to offer appropriate support versus randomly discussing this information with others.

Goals

- Strengthen interpersonal boundaries by developing discretion when discussing private information
- Discriminate between situations in which it is appropriate to discuss personal information and situations in which it might be best not to

Materials

- *Who, What, Where, and When Scenario Examples* (provided)
- Two pieces of paper
- Marker
- Tape
- Index cards
- Small candy or stickers (optional)

Advance Preparation

- On one sheet of paper, write at the top: "Appropriate Time." On another sheet of paper, write at the top: "Time to Wait." Tape the papers on opposite walls or in another manner that separates the two concepts.

- On index cards, write down at least 10 different scenarios, settings, or situations the client may encounter that would qualify as either an appropriate time to share or a time when it would be better to wait for a different context. The scenarios you choose should be based on the client's age, cultural influences, and community to reflect situations the client may actually experience. See the scenario examples list for guidance if needed.

- Optional: Write "treat," "sticker," or a smiley face on several cards. During the course of play, if a player selects one of these cards, they win a treat, sticker, or other small prize. The prospect of winning something may increase engagement and incorporates an additional component of playfulness to the technique.

---

* Intervention by Sueann Kenney-Noziska, MSW, LCSW, RPT-S™

Instructions

1. Introduce the activity by saying: "Today, we're doing an activity called 'Who, What, Where, and When.' It's all about deciding when it's okay to share personal information and when it's better to wait for a different time, place, or person to share that information with. We'll look at cards with different situations, and you'll decide if it's an appropriate time or a time to wait, then explain your choice. This isn't about keeping secrets—it's about privacy and finding the right people to support you. Ready to try?"

2. Provide an example first to help them understand. Select the first card and share your thought process out loud. For instance, the scenario "on the playground with all the other kids" might go something like this: "If I discuss my very personal, difficult problem while I'm on the playground with all the other kids around, they may not understand the situation so they probably won't be able to help me. Also, some of the kids might repeat my problem or even tease me about it. So, based on this, 'on the playground with all the other kids' is probably a time when it won't help me to talk about the problem. I think I should wait." Verbalizing this thought process helps clients understand interpersonal boundaries in regard to discussing private, sensitive information with others.

3. Have the players take turns selecting a card, determining whether the situation is a time in which discussing the identified problem is appropriate or whether it is a time in which the client should wait, and then explain why they reached that particular decision. The card is then taped onto the corresponding paper on the wall.

4. Ask process questions such as:
    -   Why do you think it might be important to wait before sharing certain information in a specific situation?
    -   How might sharing this information in a private setting, like with a therapist or a trusted adult, be more beneficial than sharing it in a public place or with other kids?
    -   What are some potential consequences of discussing private or sensitive information in public places or with other kids?
    -   How can you determine if a person is trustworthy or in a position to offer support when discussing sensitive information?

WHO, WHAT, WHERE, AND WHEN SCENARIO EXAMPLES

Appropriate Time

- Alone with my teacher who knows what's going on

- With a doctor or nurse

- With a social worker

- With a counselor

- In group counseling

- In therapy

- Alone with someone I trust in my family

- Alone with my best friend (*Note: This scenario should be thoroughly processed with the client, as this situation can fall into either category.*)

Time to Wait

- On the playground with all the other kids

- On the school bus

- In line at the grocery store

- With a stranger

- With someone I just met

- At the babysitter's with all the other kids

- In the bathroom at school

- At a birthday party

- Online with friends

- Over text

- With the lunchroom staff at school

WINNING AT LOSING

AGES: 7+ | **MODALITY:** INDIVIDUAL, GROUP, FAMILY

Introduction

This activity is designed to help clients replace negative statements with positive ones and practice appropriate reactions to losing. Using a simple card game, participants learn how to lose graciously while reinforcing positive self-talk.

Goals

- Replace negative statements with positive statements
- Demonstrate appropriate losing reactions

Materials

- Standard 52-card deck
- *Wining at Losing: Positive Statements* (provided)
- Scissors
- Colored cardstock or paper, glue, and decorative craft supplies such as markers, glitter glue, and stickers (optional)

Advance Preparation

- Photocopy the positive statements and cut them into separate strips. Lay them on the table, face down.

Instructions

1. Divide the deck of cards equally among all players, face down.

2. All players turn over the top card from their pile at the same time. The player with the lowest number loses the round. (Ace counts as one, royalty cards count as 10.) If it's a tie, place those two cards aside and draw two new cards.

3. The loser of the round picks a positive statement, reads it aloud, and keeps all cards from the round.

4. Play until all the positive statements have been read aloud. The player with the least amount of cards at the end wins the game. The other players must politely congratulate the winner.

5. Bonus points can be awarded to players who change the following negative statements into positive statements:
   - I'll never win.
   - It's no fun if I lose.
   - I always lose.
   - I'm going to cheat so I win.

- I'm a loser.
- I don't want to play if I'm losing.

6. Ask process questions such as:
   - What are some ways you can be a good sport when you don't win?
   - What did you learn about ways to handle when you lose a game?
   - Why is it important to be a good sport when you lose a game?

7. Optional activity: The client can use the art supplies to create a poster out of the positive statements.

WINNING AT LOSING: POSITIVE STATEMENTS

- Win some, lose some.

- I can have fun even if I don't win.

- I lost; it's no big deal.

- I lost; it's not the end of the world.

- Everyone loses sometimes.

- Maybe I'll win next time, maybe not.

- I can handle losing.

- It's important to be a good sport.

- I can't be the winner all the time.

- Other people will enjoy playing with me if I'm a good sport.

- Everyone has to follow the rules of the game so it's fair for all the players.

- Just because I lost doesn't mean that I'm a loser.

- It's okay; I chose to play this game knowing I could lose.

- Other people deserve to win too.

- Winning might not be as fun if I didn't know what it's like to lose.

- Part of playing a game is knowing you could win or lose.

- I'm disappointed that I lost, but I know this feeling is temporary.

- Being a good sport means people will want to play with me again.

CHAPTER 5

Anxiety and Fears

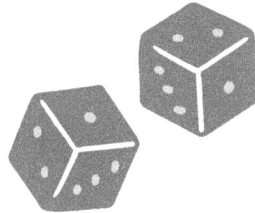

This chapter features therapeutic games designed to help children and teens understand and manage anxiety in a supportive, engaging environment. These games offer a playful yet structured way to learn about anxiety, identify anxious triggers, and replace anxious thoughts with calm and balanced thinking. By participating in these games, children can gain insight into the physical and emotional symptoms of anxiety and practice techniques to soothe the body's anxious reactions.

The interactive nature of these activities allows participants to safely confront their fears while building coping skills, resilience, and emotional regulation. Through repeated play, children can rehearse strategies for managing anxiety in real-life situations, reinforcing the idea that anxiety can be effectively managed.

The games in this chapter are tailored to provide both emotional relief and practical tools that empower children and teens to face anxiety with confidence.

BFRB BINGO*

Introduction

Body-focused repetitive behaviors (BFRBs) such as nail biting, hair pulling, and skin picking are habitual actions that often occur in response to stress or anxiety. Games can be a powerful tool in addressing BFRBs as they offer an engaging and nonthreatening way to introduce and practice coping skills. When we teach these skills through play, clients can better internalize and utilize them in real-life situations, making the learning process both effective and enjoyable.

Goals:

- Increase awareness of coping skills to decrease body-focused repetitive behaviors
- Practice coping skills

Materials

- *BFRB Coping Skills* list and *BFRB Bingo Card* template (provided)
- Scissors
- Bag
- Coloring utensils or bingo chips to cover the spaces

Advance Preparation

- Make one copy of the coping skills list and one copy per player of the blank bingo cards. (If you are planning to play with an individual client, make a copy for yourself to play!)

Instructions

1. Explain: "We are going to play a bingo game that focuses on building coping skills to help you with your body-focused repetitive behavior, or BFRB. These are habits like biting your nails, pulling your hair, or picking at your skin when you feel anxious or stressed. These actions can sometimes hurt your body and make you feel even more worried. Coping skills can help keep your hands busy, distract you from the urge, or help you deal with your feelings in a more helpful way."

2. Provide each participant with a blank BFRB bingo card and have them write a coping skill from the list in each square. They can also write their own preferred skills or ideas for new ones—just be sure to add those coping skills to your list, too!

3. Cut the coping skills into separate strips of paper and place them in a bag.

4. Explain the game: "We will take turns pulling a coping skill from the bag. Color in or place a bingo chip on the coping skills as they are called. Say 'BFRB!' when you get four in a row in any direction."

---

* Intervention by Elizabeth Ernest, LMFT, LCSW, and Laura Chackes, PsyD

5. After the game, invite the client to practice (or act out) their favorite coping skill. They can take their bingo board home as a reminder of the coping skills they can use.

6. If playing in a group, there may be multiple bingos at the same time. Explain that this is fine, since the focus is on exploring coping skills rather than on winning.

7. Ask process questions such as:
   - How did it feel to explore these coping skills through the game?
   - Which coping skill do you think will be most helpful for you and why?
   - How do you usually feel before engaging in a BFRB, and how can these skills help in those moments?
   - What challenges might you face when trying to use these coping skills outside of the game?

BFRB COPING SKILLS

- Read

- Listen to music

- Journal

- Wear stick-on nails

- Take a bath or shower

- Chew gum

- Build with LEGO

- Play a game

- Go for a walk

- Do yoga

- Call a friend or family member

- Use positive affirmations

- Draw or color

- Meditate

- Wear a hat

- Wear Band-Aids

- Track your progress

- Use fidgets

- Eat a snack

BFRB BINGO CARD

B Body	F Focused	R Repetitive	B Behavior

CANDY LAND: ANXIETY VERSION*

Introduction

In this version of Candy Land, players engage in a supportive environment where they can explore their feelings of fear and anxiety. As they move their pawns around the board, they answer questions designed to help them identify and manage their fears, as well as practice bravery and coping strategies in a playful way.

Goals

- Identify situations that correlate with anxiety
- Learn and implement coping strategies to manage anxiety

Materials

- Candy Land board game
- *Candy Land: Anxiety Version Prompts* (provided)

Advance Preparation

- Before the session, prepare a list of anxiety-related questions tailored to the needs of the client(s). Alternatively, you can use the list provided.

Instructions

1. Set up the Candy Land board as usual.

2. Players take turns picking a card from the deck. If the color on the card is different from their pawn's square or if they pick a picture card, they must answer a question from the list before moving to the appropriate square on the game board. If the card's color matches their pawn's square, they move immediately to that color and get an extra turn without answering a question.

3. Alternate version: Whenever the players land on a square that is the same color as their pawn, they must answer a question.

4. Ask process questions such as:
   - How did talking about your fears during the game make you feel?
   - What is one thing you learned today about being brave?
   - How can you use what you learned from this game the next time you feel anxious?
   - Which strategy from the game do you think will help you the most when you are anxious?

---

* Intervention by Gary G. F. Yorke, PhD

CANDY LAND: ANXIETY VERSION PROMPTS

- What is something you are afraid of? Is that real or pretend? (For example, dogs are real, while monsters are pretend.)

- Tell about a time you felt a little bit scared. Then tell about a time you felt a lot scared.

- Who can help you when you are scared?

- Being brave means doing something you are afraid to do. Being brave helps us feel better when we feel scared. Tell about a time when you were brave.

- Think of a time you were really happy. Talk about it. Pretend you are afraid and talk about the time you were really happy. Do you think that will help the next time you're afraid?

- Pretend you are afraid. Take a big breath. Blow the fear out slowly.

- You can do hard things. Pretend you feel scared, and say to yourself, "I can do hard things." Doing this when you feel scared will help you handle the situation.

- Sometimes, if a kid does not like it when their parent goes out or leaves them at school, the parent will give them something special—like an item that belongs to the parent or a keepsake the parent has made for their child. The child can hold on to this special item until their parent comes back. What kinds of items do you think would remind a child of their parent when they are apart?

- When you feel scared, it can help to say to yourself, "I am safe right now." Practice saying that.

- What advice would you give a friend to help them when they felt scared?

CLOSE FAR GAME*

AGES: 7–10   **MODALITY:** INDIVIDUAL, FAMILY

Introduction

Children with high anxiety benefit from learning about the physiological responses to anxiety. This game creates a safe environment for clients to develop an awareness of their body reactions to anxiety and normalizes these experiences.

Goals

- Identify body changes indicative of anxiety and stress
- Improve the ability to manage anxiety

Materials

- *Body Outline* and *Body Reactions* list (provided)
- Scissors
- Tape
- Blindfold
- Bag filled with small, inexpensive prizes

Advance Preparation

- Photocopy the body outline and body reactions list provided. Cut out the body outline and tape it to a smooth wall or door at a height the client can reach. Cut out each body reaction and place a small loop of tape on the back of each one.

Instructions

1. Explain: "When you are scared or worried, your body feels different. You might get a sore stomach or have diarrhea. Your body might get hot and sweaty. You might feel dizzy or even feel like you're going to throw up or faint. Your heart might beat really fast and you might have a hard time breathing. It's important to talk about what happens in your body when you are anxious or worried so you can learn ways to help your body feel better. The 'Close Far' game will help you talk about what happens in your body when you feel scared or worried."

2. Explain: "To play, stand about three feet away from the wall where the body outline is hanging and face the wall. Your parent will put a blindfold on you and place in your hand a piece of paper. The paper contains words that describe a body reaction—something that might happen in your body when you are anxious of worried. The paper has a piece of tape attached to it. Walk toward the body outline and try to stick the body reaction onto it. Your parent will say 'close' or 'far' to help you. You get two points for each body reaction that you stick onto the body outline. If you prefer, your parent can be the one wearing the blindfold, and you can say 'close' or 'far' to help them. Your parent can earn points for you!"

---

* Adapted from *Creative CBT Interventions for Children with Anxiety*, by L. Lowenstein (2016), Champion Press.

3. Continue the game until all of the body reactions have been used. At the end of the game, trade in points for prizes: 1–10 points = 1 prize; 11 or more points = 2 prizes.

4. Ask process questions such as:
   - How does your body react when you feel scared or worried?
   - Tell about a time recently when you felt anxious or worried and your body experienced an anxious reaction.

CLOSE FAR GAME: BODY REACTIONS

FAST HEARTBEAT

TIGHT MUSCLES

SORE TUMMY

DIARRHEA

HOT AND SWEATY

DIZZY

FIDGETY FEET

DRY MOUTH

TROUBLE BREATHING

CLOSE FAR GAME: BODY OUTLINE

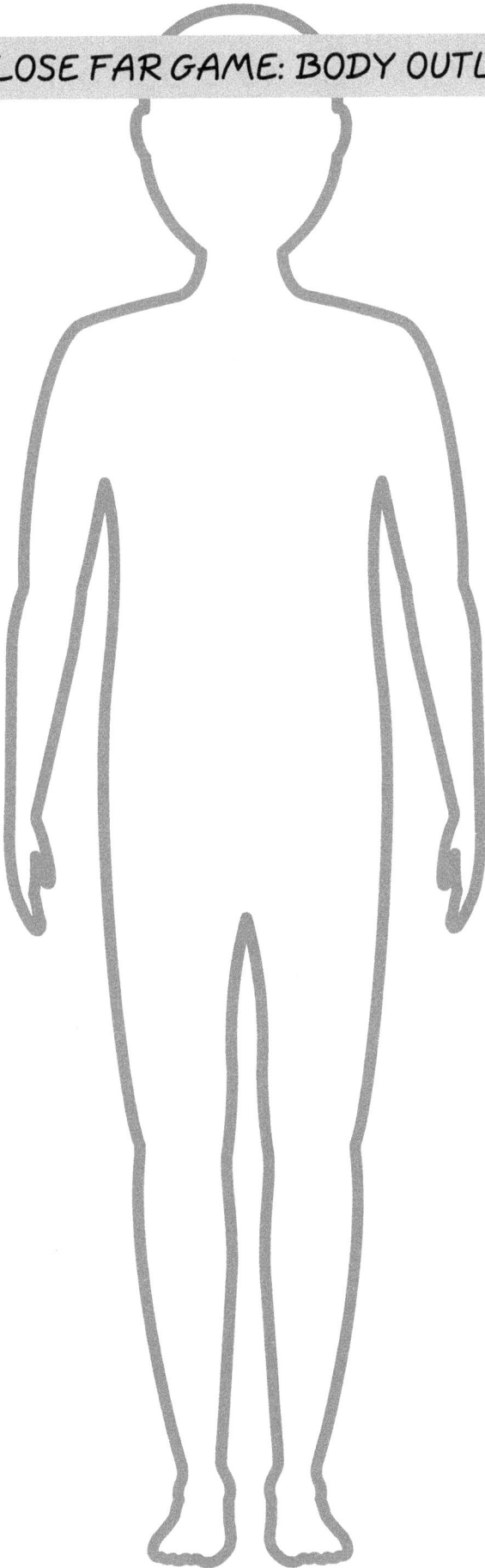

FEAR-LESS GO FISH*

Introduction

This activity uses a modified Go Fish game to help children with emetophobia (fear of vomiting). Children create their own cards featuring vomiting-related terms and practice saying the words during the game. This step-by-step exposure helps desensitize the fear response in a safe and supportive environment.

Goals

- Decrease anxiety related to fear of vomiting
- Reduce fear and avoidance of anxious thoughts

Materials

- Cardstock or colored paper
- Scissors
- Coloring utensils

Instructions

1. Teach the client a coping skill to manage anxious thoughts, such as positive self-talk (e.g., "I can handle this," "I am brave," "I can face my fears").

2. Provide psychoeducation on exposure therapy related to emetophobia. For example: "The fear of vomiting is called emetophobia. Exposure therapy helps you slowly face your fear of vomiting step by step, starting with the least scary things and working up to things that are a little scarier. Just like practicing a new skill, each time you face a small fear, you get less scared. By going slowly, you get more comfortable, and eventually, what seemed really scary doesn't bother you as much anymore!"

3. Explain that most children with emetophobia feel scared to think or talk about anything related to vomiting. Say, "We are going to create a Go Fish game with words related to vomiting, and then play the game together. This will help you think and talk about vomiting, which will help you to eventually get over your fear of vomiting."

4. Assess the client's initial level of anxiety using a subjective units of distress scale (SUDS). Explain that you will check in with the client throughout the game to see what level of anxiety they are experiencing, and that if they start to feel too scared or overwhelmed you will pause and use a coping skill together.

5. Create the Go Fish game cards with the client as follows: Cut out 16 equal-size game cards. (For a family session, increase this number by four cards per additional player.) Take turns choosing vomit-related words from the list that follows. Write each word on four separate

---

* Intervention by Elizabeth Ernest, LMFT, LCSW

cards so that each word is written four times. (If the client resists doing this, then re-explain the process and benefits of gradual exposure.)

- Throw up
- Stomachache
- Vomit
- Get sick
- Carsick
- Food poisoning
- Nausea
- Gag

- Upchuck
- Barf
- Toss cookies
- Retch
- Puke
- Queasy
- Seasick
- Spew

6. If desired, the client can decorate the cards.

7. Mix up all the cards and give each player four cards. Make sure they hide the cards in their hand from the other players. The rest of the cards stay in a central "fishing pond."

8. Have the players take turns asking another player for a card (e.g., "Do you have any 'toss cookies?'"). (Go first to model saying the word aloud for the client.) If the player asked has the card, they must give it; if not, they say, "Go fish" and the asking player draws a card from the pond.

9. When a player gets a match (two of the same word), they must say the word out loud to keep the match.

10. The game continues until all sets are completed, and the player with the most sets wins.

Note: Check in with the client throughout the activity and modify the gameplay as needed based on their current SUD rating. For example, if saying the word aloud is too scary for the client, then play an initial round in which the cards are shown or the words are whispered, then gradually work up to saying the words in a louder voice. If the client displays excessive fear, coach them to use a coping skill. Conversely, if the client is ready for a greater challenge, you can offer them bonus points for saying the word in a sentence or telling a story with all their matches.

---

11. Ask process questions such as:
    - How did you feel when you said one of the vomit-related words out loud?
    - Which word made you most anxious? Why do you think that is?
    - How did your anxiety level change from the beginning to the end of the game?
    - How did it feel to use the coping skill during the game? Did it help you manage your anxiety?

GRADUAL BALL PASS*

AGES: 3–10   **MODALITY:** FAMILY

Introduction

This activity, which is designed for family sessions, is ideal for creating safety and building a therapeutic alliance with children who suffer from selective mutism. It can also be used to build rapport with children who are very shy or anxious. The gentle, simple game helps to foster a sense of safety and connection between the therapist, parent, and child and reduce the child's anxiety in social situations. It facilitates nonverbal connection between the therapist and the child, and can progress into sound-mirroring and eventually to verbal interaction.

Goals

- Build a therapeutic alliance with children with selective mutism or with children who are very shy or anxious
- Gradually increase the child's verbal interaction with the therapist and with people outside their comfort zone

Materials

- A ball that is small enough for the client's hands and suitable for rolling back and forth

Instructions

1. Say, "Today, we're going to play a simple game with this ball that helps us get to know each other and feel more comfortable. It's not about doing it perfectly, but about having fun and taking little steps together. We'll start very easy and build from there. Let's see how it feels and take our time!"

2. The parent, child, and therapist sit on the floor in a circle.

3. Guide the parent and child through the following tasks. Repeat each task until the child demonstrates minimal anxiety (e.g., talking, smiling), and then progress to the next task. These steps may take more than one session, especially for children with selective mutism who are highly anxious about speaking to the therapist. Read each task aloud:

   - **Task 1:** The parent silently rolls the ball to the child, then the child silently rolls the ball back to the parent.
   - **Task 2:** The parent makes a sound (e.g., "beep") then rolls the ball to the child, who must copy the sound. The child then makes their own sound and rolls the ball to the parent, who must copy the child's sound.
   - **Task 3:** The parent and therapist roll the ball back and forth to each other and repeat sounds (as in the previous task), while the child observes.

---

* *Intervention by Lynn Louise Wonders, LPC, RPT-S™, CPCS, DCC

- **Task 4:** Repeat the previous task, but with the parent, therapist, and child all rolling the ball and repeating sounds. (Demonstrate delight in the child's participation.)
- **Task 5:** Repeat the previous task, but with only the therapist and child, while the parent observes.
- **Task 6:** Repeat the previous task, but while the parent leaves the room for five minutes.
- **Task 7:** Repeat the previous task while the parent leaves the room for 15 minutes.
- **Task 8:** Repeat the previous task while the parent leaves the room for the whole session.

4. Eventually, as the child begins to feel emotionally safe enough to speak, expand the game to include rolling the ball back and forth while answering simple questions about favorites (e.g., color, food, animal, book, ice cream flavor).

5. This game can be repeated at the beginning of subsequent sessions to re-engage the child and open the connectivity of the therapeutic presence and alliance.

I CAN *HANDLE* IT

Introduction
This game is designed to help children enhance their ability to cope with anxiety, discomfort, and uncertainty. By normalizing typical anxiety responses, the game fosters resilience.

Goals
- Improve the ability to manage anxiety, discomfort, and uncertainty
- Normalize common anxiety reactions

Materials
- Colored cardstock
- Scissors
- Paper
- Coloring utensils
- One die

Advance Preparation
- Prepare a list of five scenarios tailored to the client's needs, focusing on helping them manage anxiety, discomfort, and uncertainty. For example, for a client dealing with generalized anxiety disorder and perfectionism, you might write: "Imagine you're drawing and make a mistake. You feel the urge to start over. Instead, take a deep breath and tell yourself, 'I can HANDle making mistakes.'" Number the scenarios 1–5.

Instructions
1. Have the client trace their hand on the colored cardstock and cut it out to be the game board.

2. On the palm, have them write, "I can HANDle it!" Have them label the fingers with the numbers 1 through 5, starting with the thumb.

3. Have the client roll the die and respond to the scenario corresponding to the number rolled. If they roll a 6, say, "You get to create your own new scenario! Think of a time when you felt anxious or uncomfortable and explain how you would handle it by saying, 'I can HANDle . . .'"

4. If they roll a number they've already responded to, they will roll again. Continue until they've addressed all five scenarios, then encourage them to give themselves a high five with the cardstock hand.

5. Ask process questions such as:
   - How did it feel to think of ways to HANDle your anxiety?
   - Which scenario felt the hardest to HANDle, and why do you think that is?
   - What did you notice about your ability to HANDle situations by the end of the game?
   - What did you learn from the game that can help you better manage your anxiety?

LAUNCH YOUR WORRIES AWAY*

Introduction

This activity helps clients articulate their anxieties, fears, or worries. Through crafting a "worry launcher," participants can visually and physically release their worries while discussing coping strategies in a supportive setting.

Goals

- Verbally articulate anxieties, fears, or worries
- Identify coping strategies for feelings of anxiety, fear, or worry

Materials

- Paper
- Tape
- Disposable paper cup (one per client)
- Balloon (one per client)
- Coloring utensils and craft supplies
- Scissors
- *Coping Skills* list (provided on page 290)

Instructions

1. Explain to the client that when we use healthy coping skills, our anxiety lessens, or gets "launched" away.

2. Have the client write down at least three worries, anxieties, or fears on a piece of paper with some space between each one. Invite them to cut out each one into any shape.

3. Help the client make their own unique worry launcher (or you can prepare it ahead of time):
   - Cut out the bottom of a paper cup.
   - Tie off the end of the balloon with a knot (do not blow it up), then cut off the top (not the end you blow into).
   - Stretch the open end of the balloon over the drinking end of the cup. Secure it with tape.
   - Decorate the cup.

4. Have the client read one of their worries, talk about it, then crumple it up (this symbolizes strength over the fear). Have them put the crumpled paper in the open end of the worry launcher.

---

* Intervention by Lynette Nikkel MSW, RSW

5. Have the client hold the cup in one hand, aim it, then get ready to launch the paper by pulling back the knot with the other hand. As they do so, have them share a coping strategy that helps them release the worry. (Use the *Coping Skills* list provided if needed.) Then they quickly let go of the knot to launch their worry away!

6. Optional: Have a contest to see who can launch the paper the farthest or use a target or object that can symbolize hopefulness for the client to aim at.

7. Ask process questions such as:

   - How did it feel to identify and write down your worries?

   - What was it like to launch your worries away using the worry launcher?

   - What coping strategies do you think will help you the most when you're feeling anxious or worried?

   - How can you use what you learned today in your everyday life when facing your worries?

LUCKY ROLL: ANXIETY*

AGES: 7+   **MODALITY:** INDIVIDUAL, GROUP, FAMILY

Introduction

This simple dice game helps children and families understand and manage anxiety by normalizing common reactions and teaching coping skills in an engaging way. Participants learn about anxiety's physiological responses, develop strategies to cope with it, and grow more comfortable with discussing their feelings.

Goals

- Verbalize an understanding of anxiety, physiological responses to anxiety, and coping skills
- Normalize common reactions to anxiety

Materials

- *Lucky Roll: Anxiety Questions* (provided)
- One standard die
- Small, inexpensive prizes

Advance Preparation

- Review the provided questions and omit or modify specific questions to ensure they are appropriate to your therapeutic approach and the client's level of understanding and circumstances.

Instructions

1. Explain: "This dice game will help you learn about anxiety. You will roll this die, and the number rolled reveals the points you can earn for answering the question I will ask you. For example, if you roll a 4, you will earn 4 points for answering the question correctly. If you don't know the answer, I will read the answer to you. Then you will get a second chance to answer the question and earn the points. Don't worry if you get the answer wrong the first time—the whole point of the game is to learn about anxiety, so that's why you'll get a second chance to say what you think the answer is."

2. Have the client keep rolling the die and answering questions until all the questions you selected have been answered. Then give the client an opportunity to earn 10 bonus points by saying two things they learned about anxiety. Trade points for prizes: 1-50 points = 1 prize, 51-100 points = 2 prizes, 101 or more points = 3 prizes.

---

*   Adapted from *Creative CBT Interventions for Children with Anxiety*, by L. Lowenstein (2016), Champion Press.

LUCKY ROLL: ANXIETY QUESTIONS

Question: What is anxiety?

Answer: Anxiety is a feeling of worry or nervousness. Everyone gets anxious or worried sometimes. When kids worry a lot, it can be hard for them to feel happy and enjoy certain activities. Kids need help for anxiety when they worry much of the time, and when their fears or worries stop them from having fun or doing normal activities.

Question: True or not true: Many kids feel scared or embarrassed to admit that they feel afraid, anxious, or worried a lot.

Answer: True. Many kids find it hard to admit that they're scared and worried. Some kids may think they should act tougher or that they're too old to be scared. It's important for kids to know that it's okay to have worries and fears. Admitting that you have a lot of worries and fears is the first step to getting help and feeling better!

Question: What are some common things that kids with anxiety worry about?

Answer: Kids with anxiety often worry that bad things will happen to them or to their family. They might feel afraid to be away from their parents. They might feel afraid of things like bugs, dogs, or the dark. They might feel anxious when going to parties or being around people they don't know.

Question: What does anxiety feel like in the body?

Answer: When you feel anxious or worried, you might get a sore tummy or have diarrhea. Your body might get hot and sweaty. You might feel dizzy or shaky, or even feel like you're going to throw up or faint. Your heart might pound really fast and you might have a hard time breathing. Therapy can help you learn ways to handle anxiety so your body doesn't feel so bad.

Question: What is the fight, flight, freeze response?

Answer: When a person thinks that something dangerous is about to happen, their body makes chemicals that get them to **fight** off the danger, or run away from the danger (**flight**), or get very still (**freeze**). The fight, flight, freeze response can protect you when there is real danger, but it can be a problem when there is no real danger. For example, let's say you are afraid of dogs. You are at the park and you see a dog. The dog is not doing anything dangerous. But because you are afraid of dogs, you think this dog is dangerous. You might do something like hit the dog with a stick (fight), or run away from the dog (flight), or feel unable to move (freeze). Therapy can help you learn ways to tell your brain and body to react differently so you can cope better with scary situations.

Question: True or not true: Some anxiety can be helpful.

Answer: True. Anxiety can actually be helpful because it can protect people from real danger. For example, if you're crossing the street and a car comes fast toward you, anxiety will alert you to this danger so you can get out of the car's way.

Question: What is the role of a therapist in helping with anxiety?

Answer: A therapist helps by providing support, teaching coping skills, helping to identify and change negative thought patterns, and guiding gradual exposure to feared situations.

Question: True or not true: Therapy is only for people with severe anxiety.

Answer: Not true. Therapy can be helpful for anyone experiencing anxiety, regardless of its severity. Therapy provides tools and strategies to manage anxiety and improve overall mental health.

Question: What is cognitive behavioral therapy (CBT)?

Answer: Cognitive behavioral therapy, or CBT for short, is a type of therapy to help people with anxiety. In CBT, kids learn special skills to help them cope with worries and fears. CBT has proven to be the best way to help kids deal with anxiety.

Question: What are some healthy ways to cope with anxiety?

Answer: Some healthy coping methods include deep breathing, mindfulness, exercising regularly, getting enough sleep, eating a healthy diet, and talking about your worries with someone you trust.

Question: True or not true: Avoiding things that make you anxious can help reduce anxiety in the long run.

Answer: Not true. Avoiding things that make you anxious might help you feel better in the short term, but in the long run, it can make anxiety worse. Facing your fears gradually can help reduce anxiety over time.

Question: What role do thoughts play in anxiety?

Answer: Thoughts can play a big role in anxiety. Negative or unrealistic thoughts can increase anxiety, while positive or realistic thoughts can help reduce it. Therapy can help you learn to identify and change negative thoughts.

Question: How can exercise help with anxiety?

Answer: Exercise can help reduce anxiety by releasing endorphins, which are chemicals in the brain that act as natural painkillers and mood elevators. Exercise also helps by improving sleep, reducing tension, and increasing overall well-being.

Question: What is mindfulness and how can it help with anxiety?

Answer: Mindfulness is paying attention to the present moment without judgment. It can help with anxiety by making you more aware of your thoughts and feelings, helping you to respond to them in a calm and thoughtful way rather than reacting impulsively.

Question: How can keeping a journal help with anxiety?

Answer: Keeping a journal can help with anxiety by allowing you to express your thoughts and feelings, track your progress, identify patterns in your anxiety, and develop strategies to manage it.

Question: What is gradual exposure?

Answer: Gradual exposure is part of CBT. Gradual exposure involves facing a fear a little at a time until the fear is not so scary anymore. Don't worry—we will only start this part of therapy when you are ready. We will make a plan together so you feel okay with it. After a while, your anxiety will lessen and you will feel calmer and better.

Question: True or not true: The goal of therapy is to make anxiety go away.

Answer: Not true. Remember, some anxiety is normal and helpful, so we need a certain amount of anxiety. The goal of therapy is to help kids handle fears and worries so anxiety does not stop them from having fun or from doing normal activities.

Optional Questions
(Only include if appropriate for the client)

Question: What is separation anxiety?

Answer: Separation anxiety is when children feel really scared to be away from their parents. They may get scared when their parents leave them with a babysitter or when they're dropped off at a friend's home. Therapy will help you learn ways to handle being away from your parent(s) so you don't miss out on fun, and so you can feel calmer and happier.

Question: What is social anxiety?

Answer: Kids who have social anxiety feel really scared when they are around people they don't know well. This makes it hard for them to meet new people, go to parties or camp, or join a team. Therapy will help you learn ways to feel safe around people you don't know well.

Question: What is selective mutism?

Answer: Selective mutism is when a child does not speak in some situations but speaks comfortably in other situations. Kids with selective mutism might not speak at school or around people they don't know well, but they're usually comfortable speaking at home.

Question: What is a phobia?

Answer: A phobia is an extreme fear to a thing or a situation. The thing or situation is not actually as dangerous as the person thinks it is. But to the person with the phobia, the danger feels real because the fear feels so huge. Phobias cause people to worry about and avoid the things or situations they fear. Having a phobia can stop you from enjoying normal activities. Therapy will help you learn ways to deal with your phobia.

Question: What is obsessive-compulsive disorder (OCD)?

Answer: OCD causes someone to have worrying thoughts (obsessions) or repeated behaviors (compulsions) that they don't want but cannot stop, no matter how hard they try. Therapy will help you learn ways to get control over OCD.

Question: What is a panic attack?

Answer: A panic attack is when the anxiety gets so strong that it seems to take over your whole body. For example, you can have a hard time breathing. You might also notice that your heart beats faster and you feel dizzy or sweaty. Therapy can help you learn to handle and even prevent panic attacks.

POP-UP GAME

Introduction

This intervention emphasizes that we can tolerate discomfort even when we feel anxious by encouraging players to recognize and verbalize their physiological responses to sudden anxiety-inducing events within the game. Through repeated play and the practice of self-talk, children learn to affirm their ability to handle these uncomfortable feelings, reinforcing the concept that everyone experiences anxiety at times, but with the right strategies, they can manage and tolerate these sensations effectively.

Goals

- Verbalize common physiological responses to anxiety
- Learn, practice, and utilize appropriate self-talk to manage anxiety

Materials

- A board game that pops up, such as Pop-Up Pirate or Perfection

Instructions

1. Play the pop-up board game in the usual way, then discuss the following:
   - How did you feel when the game suddenly popped up? (Emphasize how you both felt scared, anxious, and/or uncomfortable.)
   - How did your body react when the game suddenly popped up? (Emphasize common physiological responses to anxiety using language that the child will understand, such as "Our bodies jump or twitch, our heart rate speeds up, and our muscles get tighter.")
   - Tell me about some other times when you felt scared, anxious, or uncomfortable (Normalize that everyone at times feels scared, anxious, and uncomfortable.)

2. Say, "Everyone feels scared, anxious, and uncomfortable sometimes. Learning to tolerate feeling scared, anxious, and uncomfortable is a helpful skill, as it will help you cope better with these feelings and reactions. One helpful strategy is self-talk—for example, saying to yourself, 'I don't like this anxious feeling, but I can handle it,' or more simply, 'I can handle this.'"

3. Play the game again, but this time, use self-talk. For example, before the game, both of you say to yourselves, "It's going to pop up and I'll feel scared, but I will be able to handle it." After the game, say to yourselves, "I handled it."

4. Invite the client to make a list of situations that make them feel anxious, and help them identify how they can use self-talk to help them manage their anxiety in real-life situations.

SUPERHERO DICE*

Introduction

This game is designed to help children identify their anxious thoughts, understand their physical reactions to anxiety, and develop coping skills in an engaging way.

Goals

- Identify worries, fears, and anxious thoughts
- Increase understanding of the physical reactions to anxiety and identify which ones the client experiences
- Implement coping skills to manage anxiety

Materials

- *Superhero Dice Questions* list (provided)
- One die

Instructions

1. Explain: "To learn more about anxiety, and how we can be brave and face our worries and fears, we are going to play a game where we are superheroes! You will roll the die and answer the question that corresponds with the number rolled. For example, if you roll a 1, you will answer question 1. The questions will help you talk about worries, fears, and anxiety."

2. Take turns rolling the die and answering the corresponding question from the list provided. If a player gets a number they have previously rolled, they should roll again until they get a new question. Continue until the client has answered all six questions.

3. Ask process questions such as:
    - How did you feel while answering the questions about your worries and fears?
    - Did any of the questions make you think differently about your anxiety? If so, how?
    - How can you use what you learned in this game to manage your anxiety in real life?
    - What was the most helpful part of the game for you, and why?

Variations

- **Incorporate actionable superhero skills:** Add a physical component where the player must act out a superhero action related to their answer. For example, after answering the superhero body scanner question, the player can pretend to engage their superhero powers (e.g., deep breathing, flexing muscles) to calm down.

---

* Intervention by Lauren Mosback, LPC, NCC

- **Use superhero mission cards:** Create mission cards and have the players draw a card after answering a question. Each card offers a small task related to facing anxiety (e.g., "Use your superhero powers to think of one way to calm down when feeling scared").
- **Add an obstacle:** Create an additional step where rolling a specific number means the child faces an obstacle, which introduces a challenge related to anxiety. They have to use one of their superhero coping skills to overcome it. For example: "You are facing a storm of worries! Use your superhero breathing to stay calm and roll again!"
- **Introduce a collaborative element:** For group settings, players could work together to help each other with their worries, brainstorming strategies as a "superhero team."

SUPERHERO DICE QUESTIONS

- If one of your superhero abilities was the power to erase any worry from your mind, which worry would you choose to erase? Why?

- When you're feeling anxious, imagine you have a superhero body scanner. What does the scanner show about how your body feels? What are the signs that your superhero body is experiencing stress?

- Think of a time when you, as a superhero, faced one of your biggest worries. What was the challenge, and how did your superhero self handle it? What happened next?

- What is your greatest fear that even your superhero self finds challenging? How would your superhero alter ego face this fear?

- Name a superhero you admire for their bravery. What makes them so brave, and how can you use their bravery as inspiration when facing your own fears?

- Imagine you have a special superhero toolkit for calming down. What coping skills or self-care strategies would be in your superhero toolkit to reduce anxiety? How would you use them to help yourself or others?

CHAPTER 6

Trauma and Other Stressful Life Events

In this chapter, the focus is on how therapeutic games can provide a safe and structured space for children and teens to process their traumatic and difficult experiences. Trauma can create overwhelming emotions and a sense of disconnection, and games offer a nonthreatening way for young people to express feelings they may struggle to articulate in traditional talk therapy.

Through gameplay, children and teens can externalize their inner worlds, opening up conversations about difficult life events in a more manageable and less intimidating way. Games provide a way to safely explore different emotions, build resilience, and foster post-traumatic growth. Additionally, they can enhance therapeutic rapport, provide psychoeducation, and promote emotional healing in a playful, supportive environment.

"CAUGHT IN THE MIDDLE" SCRIBBLE TAG*

Introduction

This game helps children of divorce express and process their feelings of being caught in the middle of their parents. By using the game to symbolize the back-and-forth tension between parents, children can safely explore these emotions in a playful and nonthreatening way. The physical act of trying to "catch" or avoid being "caught" mirrors their emotional experience, providing a fun yet insightful means to verbalize and discuss their feelings about the divorce.

Goals

- Normalize that children of divorce often feel caught in the middle
- Help the client verbalize feelings related to the divorce

Materials

- Large sheet of durable paper or whiteboard
- Two different colored markers

Instructions

1. Explain the game:
   - Children often feel caught in the middle when their parents divorce. This is because their parents are fighting and they are in the middle of it. This game will help you talk about these feelings.
   - To play, we will sit on the floor with a large sheet of paper between us. On one end of the paper, write *MOM*, and on the other end, write *DAD*. In the middle of the paper, write *MIDDLE* in big letters.
   - We will each use a different color marker. This game is played like tag, but instead of tagging people, players tag markers. The object of the game is for the person who is "It" to catch the other player's marker with their marker. "It" must scribble fast to catch the other player's marker, while the other player must scribble fast so their marker does not get tagged or caught by It. You get to decide which player is going to be It.
   - We will place the tips of our markers down on the paper. Once the round begins, we must scribble with our markers as fast as we can, and we cannot lift our markers off the paper until it catches the other player's marker with their marker. Then we will change roles so the other player is It.

2. Ask process questions such as:
   - How come children of divorce often feel caught in the middle?
   - How does it feel for a child to be caught in the middle?
   - What ideas do you have about how children can cope better with these feelings?

---

* Adapted from *Creative Interventions for Children of Divorce,* by L. Lowenstein (2006), Champion Press.

I SPY SOMATIC SAFETY*

AGES: 8+   **MODALITY:** INDIVIDUAL, GROUP, FAMILY

Introduction

This game is designed to help children and adolescents who have experienced trauma to learn how to manage their bodily symptoms effectively. Trauma triggers can appear in different forms, often affecting the body and nervous system. The primary goal of this game is to help clients feel safe and comfortable within their own bodies.

Goals

- Learn and utilize techniques to calm the nervous system
- Facilitate the release of trauma that may be stored in the body through playful somatic experiences

Materials

- *I Spy Somatic Safety* cards, picture search, and tally sheet (provided)
- Scissors
- Coloring utensils

Advance Preparation

- Make a copy of the *I Spy Somatic Safety* cards, picture search, and tally sheet.
- Cut out the cards and select or modify them as needed so they are appropriate to your client. Note that some require additional materials and preparation (e.g., creating a sensory glitter jar that the client can shake). You can also create some blank cards for the client to add their own activities.

Instructions

1. Explain how trauma can be stored in the body's nervous system. Use metaphors to illustrate the concept. For example, you could say:
   - Think about your body like a big balloon. When something scary or upsetting happens, it's like someone is blowing air into the balloon. The balloon gets bigger and bigger with each upsetting thing, even if you try to ignore it. If the balloon keeps getting filled up with air but never gets a chance to let any air out, it might start to feel tight and uncomfortable. You might feel jumpy, have a hard time relaxing, or get upset easily.
   - But just like you can slowly let air out of a balloon so it doesn't pop, you can let out the uncomfortable feelings from your body. You can talk about what happened with a safe person, take deep breaths, or do something else that makes you feel safe and calm. These strategies help let out some of the "air" and make the balloon softer and easier

---

* Intervention by Niki Picogna, PsyD, LCPC, LPC, LMHC, RPT-S™

to handle. Over time, if you keep letting out a little air, you will feel more comfortable in your body again.

2. Engage in the playful somatic safety exercises written on the game cards you selected. This can be done across multiple sessions before introducing the I Spy game.

3. Present the I Spy picture search and tally sheet. Explain the instructions: "Find each object in the picture and count how many you can spot. Write down the number of times you see each item next to it on the list. As you find each item, take a moment to notice how it makes you feel in your body."

4. Ask process questions such as:
   - What was your favorite somatic safety skill and why?
   - How can this game help you and your body feel safer or more relaxed?

5. Provide the client with a copy of the cards and picture search to take home, where they can color the pictures and continue practicing the somatic safety skills.

"I SPY SOMATIC SAFETY" CARDS

Cold Water
Drink some cool water, or splash it on your face or neck.

Birthday Candle Breathing
Take a deep breath in through your nose like you're smelling your birthday cake… then blow out the candles!

Glitter Jar
Gently shake the jar and watch the glitter swirl.

Go Outside
Sit or take a walk outside and notice the natural world around you.

Essential Oil
Find a scent that calms you.

Rocking
Gently rock your body back and forth, or swing on a swing.

Drumming
Play a soothing rhythm on a drum or with your hands.

Butterfly Hug
Cross your arms over your chest and gently tap your fingertips against your collarbone, alternating left and right.

Soothing Sensations
Pick a small item—like beads, a stress ball, or a smooth stone—and notice how it feels in your hands.

Snapshot Body Scan
Imagine you are taking a picture of each part of your body, starting with your head and going down to your toes. What do you feel in each part?

Dance

Move your body in any way that feels good—it can be silly if you want!

Bee Breathing

Take a deep breath in through your nose, then breathe out through your mouth while buzzing like a bee.

Scribble

On a piece of paper, scribble a long, smooth zigzag from left, to right, to left, to right…

Bubble Bath

Take a peaceful bubble bath (or imagine you are taking one). What scents and sensations do you notice?

Feel Your Heartbeat

Place your hand over your heart and notice how it beats as you breathe slowly in and out.

Stretching/Yoga

Practice some stretches or yoga poses that you have learned and notice how your body feels.

Eat Something Crunchy

Mindfully munch on a crunchy snack, like carrots or almonds.

Walking

Take a walk (outside, if you can). What do you sense within and around you?

Listen to Music

Play your favorite songs and notice how your body feels.

Figure Eight Breathing

Start at the center. Trace one half of the figure as you breathe in for 1, 2, 3, 4 until you reach the center, then breathe out for 1, 2, 3, 4 along the other half.

"I SPY SOMATIC SAFETY" PICTURE SEACH

"I SPY SOMATIC SAFETY" TALLY SHEET

How many times can you find each item in the picture search?

(drink with ice)	_____	(person dancing with music notes)	_____
(jar with stars)	_____	(bee)	_____
(essential oil bottle with flower)	_____	(crayon)	_____
(drum)	_____	(bathtub with bubbles)	_____
(leaf/seed)	_____	(stethoscope)	_____
(candles)	_____	(person on hands and knees)	_____
(sun)	_____	(carrot)	_____
(rocking chair)	_____	(person walking)	_____
(butterfly)	_____	(headphones with music note)	_____
(camera)	_____	(infinity symbol)	_____

LUCKY ROLL: BEREAVEMENT*

AGES: 7+   **MODALITY:** INDIVIDUAL, GROUP, FAMILY

Introduction

This game is designed to help clients explore feelings about death and the grieving process. The game element allows children to learn about complex concepts such as loss, death, and grief in a more accessible and engaging way. Through answering questions and earning points, participants are encouraged to express their thoughts and emotions, helping to normalize their reactions to death.

Goals

- Verbalize an understanding of key concepts related to death and grief
- Normalize common reactions to loss

Materials

- *Lucky Roll: Bereavement Questions* (provided)
- One standard die
- Small, inexpensive prizes
- Tablet or other device with internet access

Advance Preparation

- Review the provided questions with the caregiver prior to the session and omit or modify specific questions so they fit the family's cultural beliefs and mourning practices. For example, if the body of the person who died was buried in a casket, omit the material about cremation, and vice versa.

- Cue up some photos of the relevant places and objects (e.g., cemeteries, headstones, caskets, ashes, urns). Then, as those topics come up during the game, you can say to the client, "Let's look at some pictures of that." This helps to illustrate and normalize these places and items.

Instructions

1. Explain: "It can be hard to talk about death and upset feelings, so let's play a game to make it easier. To play, roll the die. The number rolled reveals the points you can earn for answering a question that I will ask you. For example, if you roll a 4, you will earn 4 points for answering the question correctly. If you don't know the answer, I will read the answer to you. Then you will get a second chance to answer the question and earn the points. Don't worry if you get the answer wrong the first time—the whole point of the game is to learn about death, so that's why you'll get a second chance to say what you think the answer is."

2. Have the client keep rolling the die and answering questions until all the questions you selected have been answered. Then give the client an opportunity to earn 10 bonus points by saying two things they learned about death. Trade points for prizes: 1-50 points = 1 prize, 51-100 points = 2 prizes, 101 or more points = 3 prizes.

---

* Adapted from *Creative Interventions for Bereaved Children* (2nd ed.), by L. Lowenstein (2024), Champion Press.

LUCKY ROLL: BEREAVEMENT QUESTIONS

Question: What does _dead_ mean?

Answer: _Dead_ is when the body of a person or animal stops working and can never work again.

Question: When a person dies, can their body still breathe or move or feel emotions?

Answer: When a person dies, their body cannot breathe, move, play, eat, talk, or sleep. They do not feel emotions like happy, sad, or scared, and they cannot feel hurt or pain because their body doesn't work anymore.

Question: Can a dead person come back alive?

Answer: A dead person cannot come back alive, even if we wish really hard. When a body dies, it stops working forever, and so the person who died cannot ever come back alive. You won't see the person who died alive again, but you can look at photos and talk about them.

Question: What is a casket?

Answer: A casket is a special box that holds the body of the person who died. Some people call the casket a coffin.

Question: What is a burial shroud?

Answer: A shroud is a special cloth, sheet, or blanket that wraps around the body of the person who died when they're prepared for burial or cremation.

Question: What is a viewing/visitation?

Answer: After a person dies, there may be a viewing/visitation where we can see the body of the person who died one last time. The body of the person who died may be lying in the casket. It may look like they are sleeping because their eyes are closed and they are not moving. But their eyes are closed and they are not moving because they are dead. Family and friends come to the viewing/visitation and talk to the family of the person who died. They may say nice things to try to help the family feel better. Some children go to the viewing/visitation, and some children don't go.

Question: What is a funeral/memorial service/cremation ceremony?

Answer: A funeral/memorial service/cremation ceremony is the time when family and friends come to remember the person who died. People tell stories and say nice things about the person who died. Some children go to the funeral/memorial service/ cremation ceremony, and some children don't go.

Question: What is a cemetery?

Answer: A cemetery is a place where people who have died are buried. The cemetery has headstones or footstones that families have put there to show who has died and been buried there. Each headstone has the name of the person who died. Sometimes the casket/urn is not buried in the ground but put in a building in the cemetery called a mausoleum/columbarium.

Question: Once the person who died is put in the casket, what happens to the body?

Answer: The casket holding the body of the person who died is taken to the cemetery. A hearse is a special car that takes the dead body in the casket to the cemetery. At the cemetery, the casket holding the body of the person who died is put into a deep hole in the ground and buried (covered with earth). Although it may seem strange or scary to put the dead body in a deep hole and bury it, this doesn't bother or upset the person, because dead bodies don't feel anything. They do not feel scared, and they do not feel any pain.

Question: What is cremation?

Answer: Cremation means the dead body is put into a special room that gets very, very hot. The room gets so hot that it turns the dead body into very small, soft pieces called ashes. In some cultures, the body is burned in the open air so that everyone can watch and participate in the ritual of saying goodbye to the physical part of that person. Being cremated may seem weird, scary, or gross, but the person who died cannot feel anything. It doesn't hurt because dead bodies don't feel pain or heat or cold.

Question: Where do the ashes go?

Answer: After the dead body is cremated and turned into ashes, the ashes are put into a container called an urn. The urn is buried in the ground or put in a building called a mausoleum/columbarium or kept at home. Some people scatter the ashes in a special place. People may also put the ashes in special necklaces, stones, or teddy bears or inside other things. People can do many creative things with ashes.

Question: Where do dead people go?

Answer: Death is a mystery, which means that we don't know for sure what happens after a person dies. But different cultures, families, and individuals have certain beliefs about what happens after a person dies. What do you believe happens after a person dies?

Question: Is it normal to have a lot of mixed-up feelings when someone dies?

Answer: Yes, people usually have a lot of mixed-up feelings when someone dies. These mixed-up feelings are called grief. You might feel sad, happy, angry, or guilty. You might feel sad sometimes, and at other times you might feel happy. You might feel guilty or bad about the times when you feel happy. You might have lots of other feelings. Whatever you are feeling is normal and okay. It's okay to have fun, laugh, and play even when something sad has happened. What feelings have you had since the person died?

Question: If you don't cry about the death, does this mean you didn't care about the person who died?

Answer: No. Sometimes, people who cared a lot about the person who died don't show their emotions or they don't cry about the death. There is no "right" way to feel or react when someone in your life dies. Not crying does not mean you did not care for the person who died.

Question: What if you feel angry or upset with the person who died or remember things about them that you didn't like?

Answer: No one is perfect. It is normal and okay to have different feelings about a person who died. It is even normal and okay to be upset with the person because they died. If you had a difficult relationship with the person when they were alive, then you're probably experiencing a lot of mixed-up feelings. Coming here may help you talk about your feelings.

Question: What are some ways children might react after someone dies?

Answer: Children usually have upset reactions when someone dies. Some children feel really scared and want to stay close to a safe adult. Some children feel so angry that they have a lot of outbursts, or they get stomachaches, have trouble sleeping, have bad dreams, or wet their bed. Some children have a hard time concentrating. Coming here will help you learn ways to feel better.

Question: What are some worries children may have after someone dies?

Answer: Children may worry that more bad things will happen, that they or someone else will die. Or they may worry about who will take care of them. They may have other worries. This is a place where you can talk about your worries and learn ways to handle them.

Question: What does *guilty* mean, and is it normal to feel guilty when someone dies?

Answer: *Guilty* means feeling bad about something we think we did wrong. Some children feel guilty that they didn't treat the person better while they were alive, or they think they did something wrong to cause the person to die, or they think they could have stopped the person from dying. It's important for you to know that nothing you said or did made the person die, and you cannot do anything to make the dead person come back alive.

Question: Is it normal and okay to feel relieved after someone dies?

Answer: People sometimes feel relieved when the person dies. If the person was very sick or in a lot of pain, then they might feel relieved that the person is no longer sick or in pain. Some people didn't get along well with the person and are relieved that the person has died. Some people have mixed-up feelings of happy and sad when the person dies. Whatever you are feeling is okay.

Question: Is it best to pretend to be happy so you don't make your family more upset?

Answer: Many children think that they should pretend to be happy so they don't make their family more upset. But it's okay to feel your feelings, show your feelings, and talk about your feelings. You don't need to worry about hiding your true feelings from your family, because adults can take care of themselves. Hiding your feelings will not stop an adult from grieving.

Question: Is it normal to feel scared when you are reminded of the death?

Answer: There may be things that you see, hear, or smell that remind you of the way the person died. It is normal to feel scared when this happens. Coming here will help you learn ways to cope with these scary reminders.

Question: If someone asks you about the death and you don't want to talk about it, what can you do?

Answer: It's okay to say, "I don't feel like talking about that right now." You get to decide when you talk about it and when you don't.

LUCKY ROLL: DIVORCE*

AGES: 7+	MODALITY: INDIVIDUAL, GROUP, FAMILY

Introduction

This game helps clients understand and normalize common reactions to divorce. By rolling a die and answering questions, children can learn key concepts about divorce in a supportive, interactive manner. The game emphasizes learning through second chances and offers rewards for participation and comprehension.

Goals

- Verbalize an understanding of key concepts related to divorce
- Normalize common reactions to divorce

Materials

- *Lucky Roll: Divorce Questions* (provided)
- One standard die
- Small, inexpensive prizes

Advance Preparation

- Review the provided questions and modify or omit specific questions to ensure they are appropriate for the client's age and circumstances.

Instructions

1. Explain: "This game will help you learn about divorce. To play, you will roll the die and answer questions I will ask you about divorce. The number rolled reveals the points you can earn for answering the question. For example, if you roll a 4, you will earn 4 points for answering the question correctly. If you don't know the answer, I will read the answer to you. Then you will get a second chance to answer the question and earn the points. Don't worry if you get the answer wrong the first time—the whole point of the game is to learn about divorce, so that's why you'll get a second chance to say what you think the answer is."

2. Have the client keep rolling the die and answering questions until all the questions you selected have been answered. Then give the client the opportunity to earn 10 bonus points by saying two things they learned about divorce. Trade points for prizes: 1–50 points = 1 prize, 51–100 points = 2 prizes, 101 or more points = 3 prizes.

---

* Adapted from *Creative Interventions for Children of Divorce*, by L. Lowenstein (2006), Champion Press.

LUCKY ROLL: DIVORCE QUESTIONS

Question: What is the difference between separation and divorce?

Answer: *Separation* is when parents decide they can no longer live happily together, so they decide to live separately. *Divorce* is the legal word for when parents go to court and the judge makes the end of the marriage final. Some parents who are separated or who are getting divorced continue to live in the same home until they can sort things out, like where they will live.

Question: Why do parents get divorced?

Answer: Parents get divorced because they cannot live happily together.

Question: What are some changes that might happen in families when parents get divorced?

Answer: The people in the family may start to have a lot of upset feelings. One parent might move to another home, or each parent might move to a different home. The children may have to move too. They may have to visit their parent in a new place or live sometimes in one parent's home and sometimes in the other parent's home. The amount of time they spend with one parent or both parents may change too.

Question: What can children do or say when their parents argue in front of them?

Answer: Children can politely say to their parents, "It upsets me when you argue. Please stop." Or they can go to another room, or they can say to themselves, "Even when my parents argue, they still love me."

Question: True or not true: Once parents divorce they do not get back together.

Answer: True. Once parents divorce it is usually forever.

Question: True or not true: Children from divorced families may feel sad, angry, or upset when they see other kids doing fun things with both of their parents together.

Answer: True. Kids may feel upset that their parents are divorced and they can no longer do fun things with both of their parents together. When they see other kids having fun with both parents, they may feel sad, angry, or jealous.

Question: True or not true: Children must pick sides and love one parent more than the other.

Answer: Not true. Children don't have to pick sides; they can love both their parents.

Question: True or not true: When a parent says mean things about the other parent to the child, the child should agree with them.

Answer: Not true. A better way to handle this is for the child to politely say to the parent, "It upsets me when you say mean things about each other. Please stop."

Question: True or not true: It is up to kids to send messages from one parent to the other.

Answer: Not true. It is not up to kids to send messages from one parent to the other. It is up to parents to communicate with each other about matters related to their children.

Question: True or not true: If a parent keeps missing visits with their child, it means they don't love their child.

Answer: Not true. When a parent misses visits, it is because that parent has problems that have nothing to do with love for their child. But it's okay for the child to feel disappointed, sad, angry, or any other way about their parent missing visits, and it's okay for the child to talk about these feelings.

Question: True or not true: Children from divorced families may think their family is weird.

Answer: True. Children from divorced families may think their family is weird. But it's important for kids to know that there are many different types of families. Some kids live in families with only one parent. Some kids live in families with parents who are separated. Some kids live in two homes. Some kids live with their grandparents or other adults who take care of them instead of their parents. There are so many different types of families!

LUCKY ROLL: INTIMATE PARTNER VIOLENCE

AGES: 7+   **MODALITY:** INDIVIDUAL, GROUP, FAMILY

Introduction

Through this game, children learn about the dynamics of intimate partner violence in a safe and structured manner. By answering questions and engaging in dialogue, participants can better understand key concepts, normalize common emotional reactions, and develop coping skills.

Goals

- Verbalize an understanding of key concepts related to intimate partner violence
- Normalize common reactions to intimate partner violence

Materials

- *Lucky Roll: Intimate Partner Violence Questions* (provided)
- One standard die
- Small, inexpensive prizes

Advance Preparation

- Review the provided questions and modify or omit specific questions to ensure they are appropriate for the client's age and circumstances.

Instructions

1. Explain: "This game will help you learn about intimate partner violence. To play, you will roll the die and answer questions I will ask you about intimate partner violence. The number rolled reveals the points you can earn for answering the question. For example, if you roll a 4, you will earn 4 points for answering the question correctly. If you don't know the answer, I will read the answer to you. Then you will get a second chance to answer the question and earn the points. Don't worry if you get the answer wrong the first time—the whole point of the game is to learn about intimate partner violence, so that's why you'll get a second chance to say what you think the answer is."

2. Have the client keep rolling the die and answering questions until all the questions you selected have been answered. Then give the client an opportunity to earn 10 bonus points by saying two things they learned about intimate partner violence. Trade points for prizes: 1–50 points = 1 prize, 51–100 points = 2 prizes, 101 or more points = 3 prizes).

LUCKY ROLL: INTIMATE PARTNER VIOLENCE QUESTIONS

Question: What is intimate partner violence?

Answer: Intimate partner violence is when one person uses power to control their partner or spouse through words, feelings, physical actions, money, or sex. Kids may see or hear physically violent actions, or they may see bruises or other evidence after the violence is over, or they may know one parent is afraid of another adult in their house.

Question: What is a perpetrator?

Answer: A perpetrator is a person who commits a crime. Using words, feelings, physical actions, money, or sex to control another person is against the law and is a crime.

Question: What are some feeling kids may experience when they have seen hurting happen in their family?

Answer: Kids may feel sad, mad, or scared. They may feel like something they did or said caused the violence. Or they may be mad at a parent or sibling for saying or doing something that they think caused the violence. Talking about feelings helps kids feel better.

Question: How come kids may feel like they caused the violence?

Answer: Sometimes parents are arguing about kids when the violence starts or kids may feel like what they did or said caused the violence. But kids are too young to make their parents or other adults do anything. That's why the violence is never a kid's fault, no matter what.

Question: What might kids worry about if they've been exposed to violence?

Answer: Kids may worry about bad things happening. They may always be on guard, waiting and watching for the next bad thing. Since they don't know what will trigger the next violent outburst, they may never feel safe or relaxed. They may worry for themselves, a parent, or their siblings.

Question: How come kids don't tell somebody about the violence?

Answer: Kids who grow up with violence in the home are expected to keep the family secret. Sometimes they don't even talk to each other about the violence. Even the parent who is hurt by the violence may be afraid to talk to anyone about it. But talking about it will help you feel better.

Question: How do children feel about the perpetrator?

Answer: Some children are angry at the perpetrator, some still love the perpetrator, and some are angry and still love the perpetrator at the same time. There is no right or wrong way to feel—whatever they are feeling is okay.

Question: How come kids may feel like they have to fix the problems in their family?

Answer: Kids may be worried about the safety of a parent when the violence starts. Some may even try to stop the violent person from saying or doing hurtful things. It is not a kid's job to stop the fighting. The most important thing is for kids to stay safe.

LUCKY ROLL: PHYSICAL ABUSE AND NEGLECT

AGES: 7+   **MODALITY:** INDIVIDUAL, GROUP, FAMILY

Introduction

The goal of this game is to help participants understand physical abuse and neglect while normalizing their reactions to it. Through the game, children answer questions about abuse and neglect, gaining knowledge and earning points to exchange for prizes. This interactive approach encourages learning in a supportive and engaging environment.

Goals

- Verbalize an understanding of key concepts related to physical abuse and neglect
- Normalize common reactions to physical abuse and neglect

Materials

- *Lucky Roll: Physical Abuse and Neglect Questions* (provided)
- One standard die
- Small, inexpensive prizes

Advance Preparation

- Review the provided questions and modify or omit specific questions to ensure they are appropriate for the client's age and circumstances.

Instructions

1. Explain: "This game will help you learn about physical abuse and neglect. To play, you will roll the die and answer questions I will ask you about physical abuse and neglect. The number rolled reveals the points you can earn for answering the question. For example, if you roll a 4, you will earn 4 points for answering the question correctly. If you don't know the answer, I will read the answer to you. Then you will get a second chance to answer the question and earn the points. Don't worry if you get the answer wrong the first time—the whole point of the game is to learn about physical abuse and neglect, so that's why you'll get a second chance to say what you think the answer is."

2. Have the client keep rolling the die and answering questions until all the questions you selected have been answered. Then give the client an opportunity to earn 10 bonus points by saying two things they learned about physical abuse and neglect. Trade points for prizes: 1–50 points = 1 prize, 51–100 points = 2 prizes, 101 or more points = 3 prizes.

LUCKY ROLL: PHYSICAL ABUSE AND NEGLECT QUESTIONS

Question: What is physical abuse?

Answer: Physical abuse is when a parent hurts their child and causes injuries like bruises or cuts. The parent may hurt their child by hitting, slapping, pushing, kicking, or throwing objects at them. The parent may hit the child with their hand or with an object like a belt. It is never okay for a parent to physically abuse their child.

Question: Why do some parents physically abuse their children?

Answer: There are many reasons why parents may physically abuse their children, but none of them make it okay. Sometimes it is because the parent has a problem controlling their angry feelings. Sometimes it is because the parent believes that hitting their child is okay. Parents who physically abuse their children need help so the abuse never happens again.

Question: True or not true: There are okay ways and not okay ways for parents to handle their child's misbehavior.

Answer: True. All children misbehave. It's part of learning! But when a child misbehaves, there are okay ways and not okay ways for parents to handle it. Examples of okay ways include sending a child to their room or taking away a privilege, like no TV for a few days. Not okay ways to handle a child's misbehavior include anything that hurts the child, like hitting or kicking the child. Parents who physically abuse their child need help to learn okay ways to handle their child's misbehavior.

Question: True or not true: All parents get angry at their children.

Answer: True. All parents get angry at their children sometimes. It is okay to be angry, but it is not okay for parents to hurt their children. Parents who physically abuse their children need to learn ways to handle their angry feelings.

Question: What are some feelings kids may experience when they have been physically abused?

Answer: Kids who are physically abused may feel sad, scared, mad, or other upset feelings. Lots of kids who are physically abused feel like they did something wrong or they deserved to be hurt. Talking about feelings helps kids feel better.

Question: How come kids may feel like the abuse was their fault?

Answer: Kids may feel like the abuse was their fault because their parent hurt them after they misbehaved. But no matter what a child does, they never deserve to be abused. That's why the abuse is never a child's fault, no matter what! The parent who abused the child is to blame and that parent needs to get help to learn okay ways to handle their child's misbehavior.

Question: What might children worry about if they have been physically abused?

Answer: Children who have been physically abused might worry that the abuse will happen again or that something else bad will happen. Or they may worry that the parent who abused them is angry with them for telling. They might worry that the parent will be in trouble. Or they may have other worries. Therapy is a place where kids can talk about their worries and learn ways to handle their worries.

Question: How come kids don't tell somebody that they have been physically abused?

Answer: There are lots of reasons why kids are scared to tell somebody that they have been physically abused. They may worry that their parent will be mad at them or will hurt them worse for telling. They may worry about getting their parent in trouble. They may think they deserved to be abused for being "bad." It's really hard for kids to tell about the abuse.

Question: What is neglect?

Answer: Neglect is when a parent does not take proper care of their child. They may not give their child enough food or they may leave their child alone. Parents who neglect their children need help to learn proper ways to take care of their children.

Question: How do children feel toward the parent who abused or neglected them?

Answer: Some children are angry at their parent, some children still love their parent, and some children feel both ways—they are angry at their parent for abusing or neglecting them *and* they still love their parent. There is no right or wrong way to feel. Whatever they are feeling toward their parent is okay.

Question: True or not true: Parents who abuse or neglect their kids do not love their children.

Answer: Not true. Most parents love their children and do not mean to hurt them. But they need to learn better ways to take care of their children.

LUCKY ROLL: SEXUAL ABUSE*

AGES: 7+   **MODALITY:** INDIVIDUAL, GROUP, FAMILY

Introduction

This intervention aims to help children understand sexual abuse, normalize their reactions, and provide a safe space to process emotions. Through an engaging dice game, children can learn key concepts about sexual abuse while earning points and prizes, promoting learning in a nonthreatening way.

Goals

- Verbalize an understanding of key concepts related to sexual abuse
- Normalize common reactions to sexual abuse

Materials

- *Lucky Roll: Sexual Abuse Questions* (provided)
- One standard die
- Small, inexpensive prizes

Advance Preparation

- Review the provided questions and modify or omit specific questions to ensure they are appropriate for the client's age and circumstances.

Instructions

1. Explain: "This game will help you learn about sexual abuse. To play, you will roll the die and answer questions I will ask you about sexual abuse. The number rolled reveals the points you can earn for answering the question. For example, if you roll a 4, you will earn 4 points for answering the question correctly. If you don't know the answer, I will read the answer to you. Don't worry if you get the answer wrong the first time—the whole point of the game is to learn about sexual abuse, so that's why you'll get a second chance to say what you think the answer is."

2. Have the client keep rolling the die and answering questions until all the questions you selected have been answered. Then give the client an opportunity to earn 10 bonus points by saying two things they learned about sexual abuse. Trade points for prizes: 1–50 points = 1 prize, 51–100 points = 2 prizes, 101 or more points = 3 prizes.

---

* Adapted from *Cory Helps Kids Cope with Sexual Abuse: Playful Activities for Young Children,* by L. Lowenstein (2014), Champion Press.

LUCKY ROLL: SEXUAL ABUSE QUESTIONS

Question: What is sexual abuse?

Answer: Sexual abuse is when someone touches a child's private body parts—such as their vagina, breast, penis, or bottom—in a way that scares them or hurts them, or when someone makes a child touch them on their private body parts. It is also sexual abuse when a child feels uncomfortable or bad because an adult or older child has shown them their private body parts, or has shown them pictures of naked people, or has made the child show their private body parts.

Question: What is a sexual abuser?

Answer: The person who sexually abuses a child is called a sexual abuser. The abuser can be a stranger or someone the child knows. The abuser might be mean and hurtful, or the abuser might be nice and friendly or even give the child a gift or treat. Kids may be angry or scared of the abuser, or they may still like or love the abuser—or they may have all of these different feelings at the same time, which can be confusing. Whatever kids feel toward the abuser is normal and okay.

Question: Why do people sexually abuse kids?

Answer: It's hard to understand why anyone would sexually abuse kids. Some people have sexual feelings for children that most people don't have. Abusers know that sexual abuse is wrong, but they do it anyway because it feels good to them. Abusers trick or force kids to make them feel confused or scared so they will go along with the sexual abuse and not tell anyone. Even though there are some people who sexually abuse kids, there are *many* more people who only touch kids with good, okay touches.

Question: Who is sexually abused?

Answer: Unfortunately, sexual abuse happens to a lot of kids. It happens to children of all genders, ages, and ethnicities. The important thing to remember is that sexual abuse is never the child's fault. Nothing a child said or did made the sexual abuse happen. Sexual abuse doesn't happen because of what a child looks like, or because of what a child was wearing. Sexual abuse is *always* the abuser's fault.

Question: What is a trauma?

Answer: A trauma is when something really bad happens and it makes someone feel very scared. Sexual abuse is a trauma.

Question: What is a trauma trigger?

Answer: A trauma trigger is something that reminds a person of the trauma and makes them feel scared. A trauma trigger might be a person or place or even a smell or sound, or anything else that reminds them of what happened. Therapy helps kids learn ways to deal with trauma triggers.

Question: What are some common feelings that kids experience when they have been sexually abused?

Answer: Each child who is sexually abused responds to it in their own way. But there are common feelings that children may experience, like confused, sad, angry, embarrassed, and scared. Many kids feel guilty because they think the sexual abuse was their fault. Lots of kids who are sexually abused feel like they did something bad or that they will be blamed for it. Therapy is a place to talk about feelings and learn ways to feel better.

Question: What are some problems kids may experience when they have been sexually abused?

Answer: Kids who are sexually abused often have nightmares or scary memories of the abuse that pop into their head during the day. They may feel very nervous and jumpy and not know why. Some kids feel so angry that they lose their temper a lot. Some kids feel so scared or worried that they get frequent stomachaches or headaches. Children who go to therapy get help for these problems and learn ways to feel better.

Question: What might children worry about if they have been sexually abused?

Answer: Children who have been sexually abused might worry that the sexual abuse will happen again or that something else bad will happen. They may worry that the abuser is angry at them for telling. Or they may have other worries. Therapy is a place where kids can talk about their worries and learn ways to cope with their worries.

Question: How come kids don't tell somebody right away about the sexual abuse?

Answer: Kids may not tell anybody about the sexual abuse because they are scared they will get in trouble. They may think that others will not believe them. Or they may not tell anybody about the sexual abuse because the abuser told them not to tell, or threatened them. It may be really hard for kids to tell somebody about the sexual abuse.

Question: When children first tell someone about the sexual abuse, how come they may not tell about everything that happened?

Answer: Many children don't tell everything that happened to them about the sexual abuse when they first talk to someone about it because they feel scared or embarrassed. Sometimes they tell just a little bit about it to see how the person they told will react. Children usually tell more about what happened when they feel safe, comfortable, and supported, and when they know they will not get in trouble.

Question: How come kids may feel like the sexual abuse was their fault?

Answer: Kids may feel like the sexual abuse was their fault because they let the abuser touch their private body parts or because they touched the abuser's private body parts even though they knew something about it wasn't right. It is important for kids to understand that the abuser made them feel confused or scared. Sexual abuse is always the abuser's fault, no matter what!

Question: What are some reasons why it's hard for kids to stop the abuse from happening?

Answer: Kids may feel scared or confused. The abuser may use force, guilt, threats, or tricks to get them to go along with the sexual abuse. Children may feel they can't say no because they are taught to obey adults and the adult is someone they trusted. Some kids like the special way the abuser treats them, so it's hard to say no to the abuse. Therapy helps children learn ways to stay safe so the sexual abuse will not happen again.

Question: Does sexual abuse always hurt or feel bad?

Answer: Sexual abuse may hurt. But sexual abuse can also feel good. It can feel good when someone is touching your private body parts. This can be confusing. It is important for kids to know that they are not weird or bad if the sexual abuse felt good.

Question: Why do kids like the special attention they got from the abuser?

Answer: All kids like to be treated special. All kids like attention. If the abuser treated the kid nice and gave them special attention, it is normal that this felt good and it is understandable that they wanted to spend time with the abuser.

Question: Why do some parents get angry at their kids when they tell about the abuse?

Answer: The parent may be acting angry because they are so upset about the whole situation and they don't know how to handle it. They may be angry at their child for not telling right away because they don't understand how hard it is for kids to tell. Just like kids, parents feel confused about the sexual abuse and they need help to learn how to support their child. It is important for kids to know that they did not do anything wrong or bad to make their parents angry.

Question: Are children who are sexually abused weird or bad?

Answer: No, children who are sexually abused are not weird or bad, and there is nothing weird, wrong, or bad about their body. But it is common for kids to feel this way after sexual abuse. Therapy helps kids feel better about themselves and about their body.

Question: True or not true: Children who are sexually abused are messed up forever.

Answer: Not true. When children receive therapy, they can heal from sexual abuse. Many children become emotionally stronger and better able to cope with problems and challenges.

LUCKY ROLL: SUBSTANCE USE DISORDER*

AGES: 7+   **MODALITY:** INDIVIDUAL, GROUP, FAMILY

Introduction

In this activity, children will learn about substance use disorder (SUD) through an interactive approach. By rolling a die and answering questions, participants will gain a better understanding of key concepts related to SUD, while normalizing common reactions to this sensitive topic. The game encourages learning by giving participants second chances to answer questions, emphasizing that mistakes are part of the learning process.

Goals

- Verbalize an understanding of key concepts related to substance use disorder
- Normalize common reactions to substance use disorder

Materials

- *Lucky Roll: Substance Use Disorder Questions* (provided)
- One standard die
- Small, inexpensive prizes

Advance Preparation

- Review the provided questions and modify or omit specific questions to ensure they are appropriate for the client's age and circumstances.

Instructions

1. Explain: "This game will help you learn about substance use disorder. To play, you will roll the die and answer questions I will ask you about substance use disorder. The number rolled reveals the points you can earn for answering the question. For example, if you roll a 4, you will earn 4 points for answering the question correctly. If you don't know the answer, I will read the answer to you. Then you will get a second chance to answer the question and earn the points. Don't worry if you get the answer wrong the first time—the whole point of the game is to learn about substance use disorder, so that's why you'll get a second chance to say what you think the answer is."

2. Have the client keep rolling the die and answering questions until all the questions you selected have been answered. Then give the client an opportunity to earn 10 bonus points by saying two things they learned about substance use disorder. Trade points for prizes: 1–50 points = 1 prize, 51–100 points = 2 prizes, 101 or more points = 3 prizes.

---

* Adapted from *Creative Interventions for Bereaved Children* (2nd ed.), by L. Lowenstein (2024), Champion Press.

LUCKY ROLL: SUBSTANCE USE DISORDER QUESTIONS

Question: What are drugs?

Answer: Lots of people take medicine (also called drugs) when they are sick. Medicines are legal drugs, which means they are given by doctors to help people when they are sick or in pain. Stores can sell them, and people are allowed to buy them. But it's not legal, or safe, for people to use these medicines any way they want or to buy them from people who are selling them illegally. Alcohol is another kind of legal drug, but you must be a certain age to buy and drink it. Some drugs are illegal for anyone to buy and use, like ecstasy, cocaine, LSD, crystal meth, and heroin. Some people struggle with drug or alcohol use because they take too much medicine or drink more alcohol than is safe for their body, or they use illegal drugs. *Substance* is another word used for alcohol, medicine, or drugs.

Question: Why are drugs sometimes dangerous?

Answer: Taking too much medicine, drinking too much alcohol, or using illegal drugs can damage the brain, heart, and other important parts of the body. While using drugs, it's often harder to think clearly. People can do dangerous things that could hurt them, or other people, when they take too much medicine, drink too much alcohol, or use illegal drugs.

Question: Why do people misuse legal drugs or use illegal drugs?

Answer: Some people take too much medicine, drink too much alcohol, or use illegal drugs because they like the feeling it creates, even though it can harm their bodies or brains. Then, because of what those drugs do to their brains, it's very hard for them to stop taking them, even when they could die.

Question: If people get sick and take medicine, will they die too?

Answer: Medicine is almost always safe when someone takes it the way their doctor tells them to.

Question: What is substance use disorder (also called drug or alcohol addiction)?

Answer: Substance use disorder, or SUD, is a disease that makes someone use more alcohol, medicine, or drugs than is safe for their body. This disease tricks the brain into thinking that the body needs drugs or alcohol to survive. It's very hard for the person to stop using drugs or drinking alcohol even though they know they could die.

Question: What does "getting high" or "getting drunk" mean?

Answer: You may have heard the words "getting high" or "getting drunk." This means using a lot of drugs or drinking a lot of alcohol. When someone does this, it's hard for them to think properly. This can make them act weird, like being louder than normal or looking sleepy, or they may even become mean or scary. This change in their behavior doesn't mean that they are a bad person—the substance use disorder makes it hard for them to control how they behave.

Question: How might children feel when someone in their family has a substance use disorder?

Answer: If someone in a family has a substance use disorder, things at home might not feel calm or safe. Kids may feel worried, scared, sad, embarrassed, guilty, confused, or other feelings. Kids may feel angry toward the person and also still love them. All feelings are okay. Coming to therapy helps kids talk about their feelings and learn ways to feel better.

Question: What is withdrawal?

Answer: Sometimes when someone stops using drugs or alcohol after using them for a long time, their body feels upset. This is called withdrawal. It can make them feel sick, shaky, or really tired, but it gets better with time and help.

Question: What is a hangover?

Answer: A hangover happens when someone drinks too much alcohol. The next day, they might feel tired, have a headache, or feel sick to their stomach. This is their body's way of saying it didn't like all that alcohol.

Question: Do people act differently when they are drunk or high, and how might this behavior make the child feel?

Answer: People may act differently when they are drunk or high. For example, they may be more friendly or they may be mean. This change in behavior can be confusing for kids. What changes in behavior have you noticed when the person was drunk or high, and how did this make you feel?

Question: What can help a person who has a substance use disorder?

Answer: With help and support, many people can stop using substances that are dangerous for them. This is called recovery. Different recovery plans can help people with a substance use disorder. It's tricky because recovery is a decision the person has to make for themselves. No one else can make the decision for them, even if they wish really hard for it. Kids can't make the person in their life stop using substances, and it's never a kid's fault that the person has the substance use disorder in the first place.

Question: What is a substance-related death?

Answer: The term *substance-related death* is used when someone dies from using more alcohol, medicine, or drugs than is safe for their body.

Question: Why do some families want to keep it a secret if someone has a substance use disorder or dies from substance use?

Answer: Usually it's because the family is worried that others will think badly of them or the person with the substance use disorder. Sometimes children think if they talk about a family member's substance use, they will cause trouble. Therapy is a place where kids can talk about substance use in their home, and they won't get in trouble.

LUCKY ROLL: TRAUMA

AGES: 7+   **MODALITY:** INDIVIDUAL, GROUP, FAMILY

Introduction

Psychoeducation is crucial for helping traumatized children understand their experiences, normalize their reactions, and develop coping strategies. Games can engage traumatized children in a therapeutic setting by providing a safe, structured environment where they can explore their feelings and learn about trauma through play. By incorporating elements like dice rolls and points, this game helps children learn in an interactive way that encourages participation and reduces the intimidation they may feel when directly discussing difficult topics.

Goals

- Verbalize an understanding of key concepts related to trauma
- Normalize common reactions to trauma

Materials

- *Lucky Roll: Trauma Questions* (provided)
- One standard die
- Small, inexpensive prizes

Advance Preparation

- Review the provided questions and modify or omit specific questions to ensure they are appropriate for the client's age and circumstances.

Instructions

1. Explain: "This game will help you learn about trauma. To play, you will roll the die and answer questions I will ask you about trauma. The number rolled reveals the points you can earn for answering the question. For example, if you roll a 4, you will earn 4 points for answering the question correctly. If you don't know the answer, I will read the answer to you. Then you will get a second chance to answer the question and earn the points. Don't worry if you get the answer wrong the first time—the whole point of the game is to learn about trauma, so that's why you'll get a second chance to say what you think the answer is."

2. Have the client keep rolling the die and answering questions until all the questions you selected have been answered. Then give the client the opportunity to earn 10 bonus points by saying two things they learned about trauma. Trade points for prizes: 1–50 points = 1 prize, 51–100 points = 2 prizes, 101 or more points = 3 prizes.

LUCKY ROLL: TRAUMA QUESTIONS

Question: What is trauma?

Answer: Trauma is when something bad and scary happens to someone. [*Identify that what the client experienced was a trauma.*]

Question: What are some feelings kids may experience when they have been through trauma?

Answer: Kids may feel scared, sad, or angry when they think about the trauma. They may feel confused about why it happened. They may feel worried that more bad things will happen. Kids may have lots of other mixed-up feelings about what happened—there is no right or wrong way to feel. Talking about feelings helps kids feel better.

Question: What are some reactions kids may experience when they have been through trauma?

Answer: Kids who have been through trauma often have nightmares or scary memories about what happened. They may feel very nervous and jumpy. Some kids feel so angry that they lose their temper a lot. Some kids feel so scared or worried that they get frequent stomachaches or headaches. Children who go to therapy learn ways to feel better.

Question: What might children worry about if they have experienced a trauma?

Answer: Children who have experienced a trauma might worry that something else bad will happen. Or they may have other worries. Therapy is a place where kids can talk about their worries and learn ways to cope with their worries.

Question: True or not true: When a kid has experienced a trauma, they may hide their upset feelings because they don't want others to know how they really feel.

Answer: True. It is common for kids to hide their upset feelings. But it's healthier to express their true feelings rather than pretending they are okay.

Question: What is a trauma trigger?

Answer: A trauma trigger is something that reminds someone of the trauma and makes them feel scared. A trauma trigger might be a person or place, or even a smell or sound, or anything else that reminds them of what happened. Therapy helps kids learn ways to deal with trauma triggers.

Question: If a kid is asked about the trauma but they do not want to talk about it, what can they do or say?

Answer: Sometimes friends, relatives, or other people may ask about the trauma. But kids don't have to share about the trauma just because someone asks. It's okay for kids to politely say, "I don't want to talk about it." Or they can say something really brief, then change the subject.

Question: True or not true: Children who experience trauma are messed up forever.

Answer: Not true. When children receive therapy, they can heal from trauma. Many children become emotionally stronger and better able to cope with problems and challenges.

PHOTOGRAPHS AND MEMORIES: BEREAVEMENT VERSION*

AGES: 7+   **MODALITY:** FAMILY

Introduction

Continuing bonds is the process of maintaining a meaningful relationship with a loved one after their death. Talking about the person who died and preserving their memories is essential in helping the bereaved, especially children, keep a connection to the deceased. This activity fosters open communication and encourages the family to reflect on their feelings toward the person who died, creating space for healing and memory preservation.

Goals

- Discuss and preserve memories of the deceased
- Increase open communication within the family

Materials

- *Caregiver Instructions* (provided)
- *Bereavement Discussion Cards* (provided)
- Paper or cardstock
- Scissors
- One standard die
- Writing or coloring utensils
- Stapler

Advance Preparation

- Copy the discussion cards and cut them out.
- Give the caregiver the provided instructions so they can prepare the photos to bring to the session.
- Discuss with the caregiver appropriate things to say to their child during the session, when they look at the photos together. For example: "Your father and I adored you from the minute you were born," "This is our last family vacation before your father died. I feel sad and happy looking at this photo. How do you feel when you look at this picture?"

Instructions

1. Spread out all the photos and discussion cards face up on the floor.

2. The child rolls the die. If they roll an even number (2, 4, 6), they choose one of the photos to talk about with their caregiver. If they roll an odd number (1, 3, 5), they choose a discussion card and provide an answer. (Guide the child to think of memories and feelings about the person who died.) The caregiver writes the child's answer on each discussion card. Play until there are no photos or cards left.

---

* Adapted from *Cory Helps Kids Cope with Grief: Playful Activities for Young Children,* by L. Lowenstein (2024), Champion Press.

3. At the end, compile a memory book with the photos and discussion cards, using a stapler to bind the pages.

4. Ask process questions such as:
   - Point to your favorite photo in the memory book and say why it's your favorite.
   - Which photo makes you the saddest? The happiest?
   - What's something new you learned about your family from these photos?

CAREGIVER INSTRUCTIONS: "PHOTOGRAPHS AND MEMORIES" BEREAVEMENT ACTIVITY

For this activity, please prepare some family photos as described below and bring them with you to the therapy session. Each photo should be printed and taped to a separate sheet of paper. Under each photo, write a caption that includes the date and a short description (e.g., "This is your first birthday. Your father and I laughed so hard when you had your first taste of birthday cake and kept scooping more into your mouth!").

Suggested Photos

- Photo of the person who died

- Your wedding photo

- Photo of your child with their parent(s) on the day they were born or soon after their birth

- At least one photo of just your child and the person who died

- 5–8 family photos depicting holidays, birthdays, family outings, etc.

- If the person who died had a long-term illness, then it would be helpful to have some photos of the person at different stages of the illness, as this will help your child process their feelings about the illness

- 3–5 photos of special items from home or keepsakes that remind your child of the person who died

- 3–5 photos of places that remind your child of the person who died (e.g., the park where they went to play, a favorite restaurant, etc.)

BEREAVEMENT DISCUSSION CARDS

⭐ Favorite thing to do with them:

⭐ Favorite thing about them:

⭐ A funny moment with them:

⭐ A place I liked to go with them:

⭐ A family celebration:

⭐ Things they used to say:

⭐ Something kind they did:

⭐ Things we had in common:

⭐ A time I made them proud:

⭐ Something about them that I don't want to forget:

PIN THE STICKERS ON THE BODY*

AGES: 6–12

Introduction

This game is designed to help clients explore and identify the connections between their emotions and their physical sensations, particularly in the context of trauma. By visually mapping out where emotions are felt in the body, clients can gain a deeper understanding of how their experiences impact them both emotionally and physically. This game fosters self-awareness and provides a safe space for clients to articulate and process their feelings.

Goals

- Identify a range of emotions related to traumatic experiences
- Identify somatic or physiological responses related to traumatic experiences
- Verbally articulate how feelings are often stored in the body following a traumatic experience

Materials

- *Feelings Words* list and *Trauma Body Reactions* list (provided on pages 286 and 287)
- Paper
- Poster board or butcher paper
- Markers
- Scissors
- Tape
- Stickers
- Blindfold (optional)

Advance Preparation

- Create two lists: one of emotions commonly associated with trauma, and the other of physiological reactions commonly associated with trauma. (You can use the lists provided on pages 286 and 287.) Print or copy these at a large enough size that the client will be able to cut out the individual list items.

- Draw a large outline of a human body on a sheet of poster board, or trace the client's body on a sheet of butcher paper during the session. Tape the paper to the wall at the client's height.

Instructions

1. Begin by providing psychoeducation on the common emotions and physiological responses to trauma. Use the premade lists as a guide and invite the client to add to these lists. Ask the client to circle any feelings or body reactions that they experienced related to the trauma.

2. Instruct the client to cut out each emotion and physiological response that they experienced, place tape on the back, and stick it on the paper body outline. They can place it randomly or on a specific part of the body outline. Guide the client—for example, "Where in your body did you feel scared? Did you feel muscle tension mostly in your neck, shoulders, arms, or somewhere else?"

---

* Intervention by Dr. Brian L. Bethel, LPCC-S, LCDC III, RPT-S™

3. Normalize and validate the client's experience. Expand upon their statements by asking questions about each feeling/response that they report (e.g., "What happened before you felt dizzy in your head?").

4. Invite the client to play "Pin the Stickers on the Body." The client can be blindfolded or close their eyes and spin around twice (if they would like). Hand them a sticker and direct them to place it on the body outline. Once the sticker has been placed on or near one of the responses written on the body outline, discuss coping skills the client can use the next time they have this emotion or body reaction (for ideas, see the list on page 290). Add the client's preferred coping skills to the body outline.

5. This procedure can be repeated with several stickers.

6. Throughout the activity, ask process questions such as:
   - Show me where you feel _____ the most in your body.
   - What does your stomach tell you most about worry?
   - What can you do to get the _____ out of your head?
   - What strategies have worked to get the _____ feeling in a better place?
   - What can you do the next time that you feel _____ in your legs?
   - What message do your arms tell you when you feel _____ there?
   - When you feel _____ in your chest, what does that tell you about what you're experiencing?
   - How does your body react when you start to feel _____?
   - What happens in your body when you try to ignore feeling _____?
   - If the _____ feeling had a color or shape, what would it be?

TWISTED THINKING*

Introduction

This cognitive behavioral technique uses the game Twister as a format to identify and reframe distorted cognitions of guilt, blame, and responsibility for sexual abuse.

Goals

- Identify and reframe distorted cognitions of guilt, blame, and responsibility related to sexual abuse
- Decrease or eliminate self-blame for sexual abuse

Materials

- *Twisted Thinking Distorted Cognitions and Reframes* (provided)
- Twister game
- Black permanent marker
- Tape
- Circle cutter or scissors
- 48 pieces of colored cardstock (12 of each color: red, green, blue, and yellow)
- Small candies or stickers (optional)

Advance Preparation

- Review the provided list of distorted cognitions and corresponding reframes, and modify it as needed to reflect the treatment needs of the client.

- The Twister mat consists of four rows of circles arranged according to color. There are six circles in each row. Use the permanent marker to write distorted cognitions on four of the six circles in each row. Label the remaining two circles in the row with a smiley face.

- Use the circle cutter or scissors and cardstock to create two sets of covers for the mat that correspond with the color of the circle on the mat (i.e., 12 of each color: green, red, blue, and yellow). On one set of circles, write the reframe for the corresponding cognitive distortion on the mat. Set these aside. Tape the blank set of circles on top of each circle on the Twister mat to cover the distorted cognitions. It is recommended that the covers be laminated for durability.

- Place the Twister mat on the floor. Each circle on the mat should be covered to hide the distorted cognition. The reframes are grouped by color and spread out on a table or on the floor.

---

* Intervention by Sueann Kenney-Noziska, MSW, LCSW, RPT-S™

Instructions

1. Begin by discussing common thoughts of guilt, blame, and responsibility for sexual abuse.

2. Players take turns spinning the Twister spinner and removing a corresponding cover from the mat. (If the spinner lands on a color and all the covers have been removed, the player spins again.) After the cover is removed, the player reads the distorted cognition and selects the corresponding reframe from among the reframed circles. The selected reframe is taped over the distorted cognition.

3. Optional: If the player removes a cover and a smiley face is revealed, the player is awarded a candy or sticker. This may lower defenses and creates an additional level of playfulness.

4. Throughout the activity, encourage the client to discuss their own experience regarding thoughts of guilt, blame, and responsibility. Thoughts and feelings regarding the reframed cognitions are processed in relation to each client's experience.

5. Ask process questions such as:

    - How did it feel to identify and discuss a distorted cognition on the Twister mat?
    - What was the most challenging distorted cognition to reframe? Why do you think it was difficult for you?
    - How did choosing a reframe make you feel about the distorted cognition? Did it change your perspective?
    - Tell about a time outside of this activity when you felt guilt or blame that wasn't actually your fault. How might you reframe that thought now?

6. After this version of Twister is played, the group members can play the traditional version of the game if they are comfortable doing so.

TWISTED THINKING: DISTORTED COGNITIONS AND REFRAMES*

- **I should have told someone about the abuse sooner.**
  I didn't tell sooner because I was scared and confused.

- **I should have said "no" to my abuser when they abused me.**
  It was hard to say "no" because the abuser was someone I trusted.

- **It's my fault because I kept the abuse a secret.**
  I kept the abuse a secret because I was worried what would happen if I told.

- **It's my fault that my family is upset with me.**
  People can have their own feelings about what happened. It's not my fault if people are upset, and my feelings about the abuse are valid.

- **It's my fault because I knew no one was supposed to touch my private parts.**
  Even if I knew my private parts weren't supposed to be touched, it was hard to stop the sexual abuse because I was scared and didn't know what to do.

- **It's my fault my family broke up after I told about the sexual abuse.**
  My family broke up because the abuser committed a crime.

- **It's my fault because I shouldn't have trusted the abuser.**
  I was tricked or manipulated into trusting the abuser.

- **I feel guilty because the abuser got in trouble after I told.**
  The abuser got into trouble because they committed a crime, not because I told.

- **I think it's my fault because I touched the abuser too.**
  I was tricked or manipulated into touching the abuser.

- **I think the abuse is my fault because I didn't tell the abuser to stop.**
  I didn't tell the abuser to stop because I was being tricked or manipulated into going along with the sexual abuse.

---

* These distorted cognitions and corresponding reframes were guided by "Guilt Trip" in *Paper Dolls and Paper Airplanes: Therapeutic Exercises for Sexually Traumatized Children*, by G. Crisci, M. Lay, & L. Lowenstein (1998), Kidsrights.

- **I think the sexual abuse is my fault because I am a bad kid.**
  Nobody deserves to be sexually abused, no matter what. I am important and deserve to be taken care of.

- **It is my fault because sometimes my body felt good when it was being touched.**
  Some parts of my body are supposed to feel good when they are touched. That doesn't mean the sexual abuse is my fault.

- **I think the abuse is my fault because I took gifts and treats from the abuser.**
  The abuser tricked or manipulated me by giving me gifts and treats so I would go along with the sexual abuse.

- **I made the sexual abuse happen because I wore sexy clothes.**
  Nothing I wore caused the sexual abuse. The abuser is the one who caused the abuse.

- **I think the abuse is my fault because I liked being treated special by the abuser.**
  I deserve to be treated special. Treating me special did not give the abuser the right to hurt me.

- **I think the abuse is my fault because I had to go to a foster home after I told.**
  I had to go to a foster home to keep me safe, not because I did something wrong.

UPS AND DOWNS

Introduction

This intervention uses the Chutes and Ladders board game to provide a safe and engaging environment for children to explore their emotions, process difficult experiences, and learn coping strategies. By linking the ups (ladders) and downs (chutes) to therapeutic questions, this activity helps children reflect on their emotional resilience and encourages open discussion in a nonthreatening way.

Goals

- Identify and process both positive and negative emotions related to past experiences or trauma
- Utilize helpful coping strategies to manage difficult emotions
- Reflect on personal strengths, brave moments, and how helping others can promote healing

Materials

- Chutes and Ladders game
- *Ups and Downs* game cards (provided)
- Paper or cardstock in two different colors
- Scissors

Advance Preparation

- Copy the two sets of question cards—for ladders and for chutes—onto different colors of paper or cardstock (or mark the backs in some way to distinguish them). Cut out the cards.

Instructions

1. Play Chutes and Ladders using the standard rules plus one additional rule: Whenever a player lands on a ladder and moves up the game board, they draw a card from the "Ladders" set and answer the question, and whenever a player lands on a chute and moves down the game board, they draw a "Chutes" card and answer the question.

2. Ask process questions such as:
   - Tell about a time outside the game when you had a "ladder" moment—something positive that helped you cope.
   - What kinds of thoughts or feelings came up when you landed on a chute and had to answer a question about something difficult?
   - How do you think using coping strategies like those in the game can help you handle tough situations in the future?

UPS AND DOWNS: CARDS FOR LADDERS

Talking to a trusted adult about your upset feelings is a helpful coping strategy. Name a trusted adult you can talk to.

Reminding yourself that you are safe right now is a helpful coping strategy. Say to yourself: "I am safe right now."

What is something positive you've done recently that made you proud? How does it help you feel strong?

Tell about a brave moment you've had since the trauma/upsetting event happened.

Tell about a time you were kind to someone. How can helping others help you feel better about your own difficult experiences?

What helps you sleep peacefully at night? How does feeling rested affect your emotions about past trauma/ upsetting events?

Doing deep breathing is a helpful way to manage difficult emotions. Take three deep breaths.

Doing something fun can help cheer you up. Tell about a fun time you had recently.

Thinking positive thoughts is a helpful coping strategy. Say a positive thought aloud.

UPS AND DOWNS: CARDS FOR CHUTES

↓↓ Tell about a bad dream you had recently.	↓↓ Tell about a time when an upsetting memory of the trauma/upsetting event popped into your head.	↓↓ Having arguments makes you feel worse. Tell about an argument you had with someone.
↓↓ It's normal to feel angry about the trauma/upsetting event. What makes you feel angry about what happened?	↓↓ What's something that someone did that upset you since the trauma/ upsetting event happened?	↓↓ Tell about a time you didn't handle your anger well.
↓↓ It can be hard to concentrate after a trauma/upsetting event happens. Tell about a time you had difficulty concentrating.	↓↓ Having body aches is a common reaction to trauma/ upsetting events. Tell about a time when your body didn't feel good.	↓↓ Thinking negative thoughts makes you feel worse. What's a negative thought about the trauma/ upsetting event that happened?

WHIRLPOOL OF GRIEF ADAPTED IN MINECRAFT*

Introduction

This activity recreates the grief model developed by Dr. Richard Wilson within a Minecraft environment. The model adapts well to Minecraft's landscape features such as waterfalls and beaches, making it a powerful tool for exploring grief and loss. This embodied experience of navigating the grief model in Minecraft, from calm waters to the chaotic whirlpool and finally to a place of calm again, can offer valuable moments for reflection and discussion. Players experience the emotional journey in a physical way, which can deepen their understanding of grief and provide opportunities for meaningful conversations.

> **Note:** This intervention is for use with children who are familiar with and enjoy using the Minecraft video game. Therapists must be appropriately trained in the use of Minecraft in clinical settings. Using Minecraft as a therapeutic tool is not an official Minecraft product or service, nor is it approved by or associated with Mojang or Microsoft.

Goals

- Explain the stages of the Whirlpool of Grief model by Dr. Richard Wilson
- Reflect on the client's emotional experience of navigating grief

Materials

- Minecraft licenses for each player
- Computer, games console, or other device with internet access
- *The Whirlpool of Grief* model by Dr. Richard Wilson (provided)

Advance Preparation

- Become familiar with the Whirlpool of Grief model by Dr. Richard Wilson. A helpful video on implementing this intervention is available here: https://www.elliefinch.co.uk/activities

Instructions

1. Begin by explaining Dr. Richard Wilson's model of grief:
   - Imagine that we are in a boat, moving with the current down the "River of Life."
   - When we experience a loss, it is as if we are plunged over a cliff, down the "Waterfall of Bereavement." This is a shock! We might feel numb. We might have a hard time believing that the person is really gone because it all feels so sudden.

---

* Intervention by Ellie Finch, MA, MBACP (Accred.)

- The waterfall pushes us down into the "Whirlpool of Grief," where the water is spinning and churning just like all the emotions we might be feeling after the loss. We might feel sad, angry, guilty, worried, stressed, and many other mixed-up feelings.
- Because that whirlpool is spinning so fast and strong, it might push us out of the river entirely. Then we find ourselves "all washed up" on the banks of the river, feeling stuck and unable to move forward—especially if moving forward means returning to the whirlpool!
- There are also big rocks along the edge of the Whirlpool of Grief. These represent the pain of the loss, which can hit us at unexpected times as the whirlpool spins us around. Then we feel "on the rocks," which is another way of saying that we're struggling. We might have symptoms in our body, like stomachaches or feeling exhausted, as well as emotional pain.
- Fortunately, there's a way out of the whirlpool. Even though it's not possible to paddle *up* a waterfall—to go back to a time before the loss—we can steer our boat forward through the River of Life, where there will be times of calmer waters ahead of us. We do this by accepting the fact that the loss happened, and mourning and remembering the person we lost. Talking about our feelings and learning other coping skills helps us with this. Afterward, we feel more connected with our loved ones and better able to handle the rockier moments in life.

2. Next, set up this activity in Minecraft with the client as follows. Use signs to label each section of the grief model as you build:
   - **The Waterfall of Bereavement:** Locate an area with a waterfall that falls into a body of water and goes out to sea.
   - **The River of Life:** Since Minecraft does not have rivers naturally flowing into waterfalls, dig and fill a space with water at the top of the waterfall to represent the beginning of the river.
   - **The Whirlpool of Grief:** At the bottom of the waterfall, place "sponge blocks" in columns, then break them to leave a whirlpool effect in the water.
   - **All Washed Up:** On one side of the whirlpool, create a sandy beach.
   - **On the Rocks:** On the other side of the whirlpool, build a rocky area.
   - **Mourning and Acceptance:** Label the part of the river immediately following the whirlpool.
   - **The River of Life Continues:** Place this sign a bit farther down the river.

3. Set up the journey by placing a boat at the top of the waterfall in the River of Life. The client's avatar can sit in the boat and row through the different areas until they reach the calmer waters at the end.

4. Ask process questions such as:
   - What was it like being in the boat as you went down the waterfall?
   - What was it like falling into the whirlpool?
   - How does it feel to be in the calm waters again?

THE WHIRLPOOL OF GRIEF*

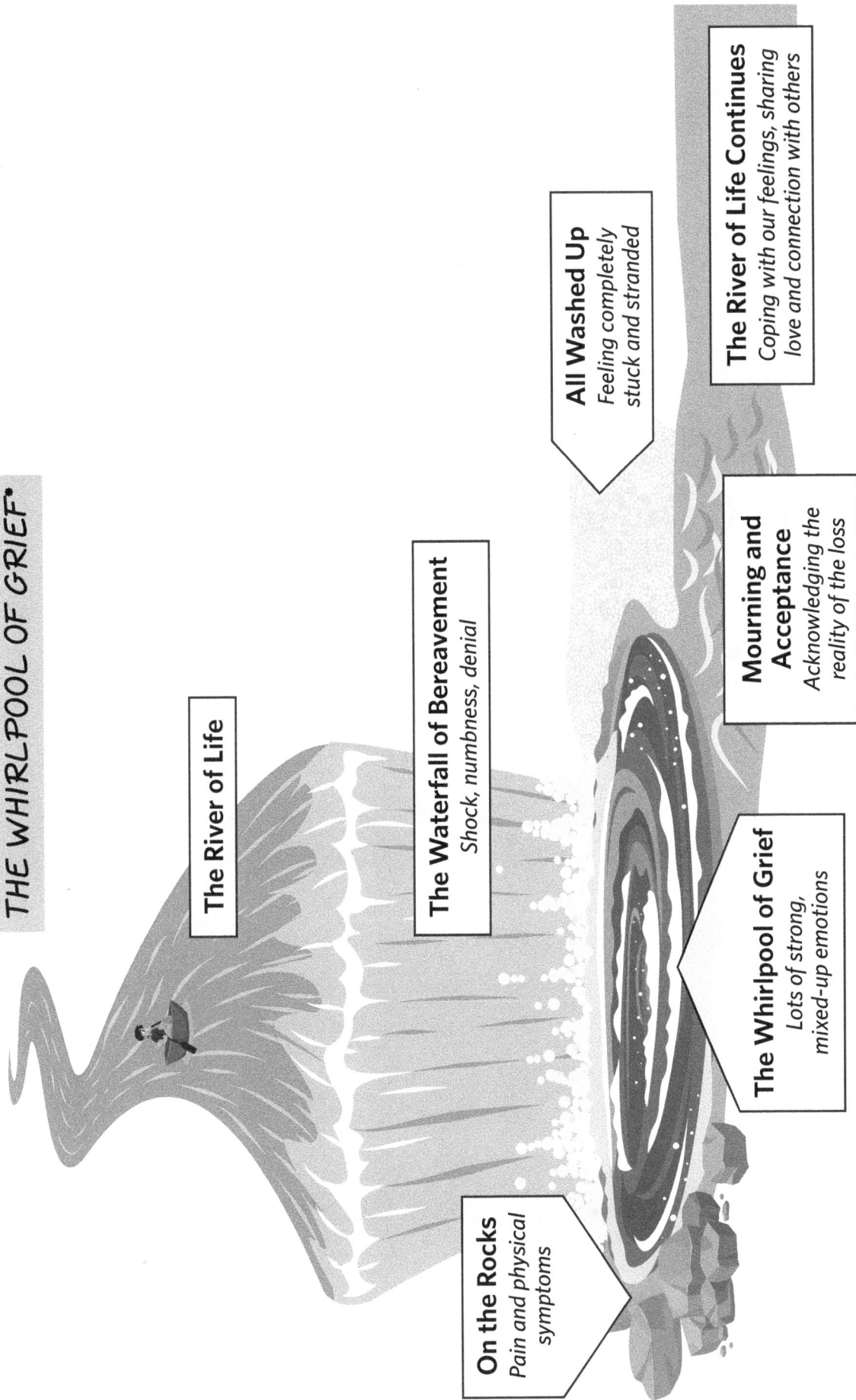

The River of Life

The Waterfall of Bereavement
Shock, numbness, denial

All Washed Up
Feeling completely stuck and stranded

The River of Life Continues
Coping with our feelings, sharing love and connection with others

Mourning and Acceptance
Acknowledging the reality of the loss

The Whirlpool of Grief
Lots of strong, mixed-up emotions

On the Rocks
Pain and physical symptoms

* Adapted from "The Whirlpool of Grief", by R. Wilson, in B. Ward et al., *Good Grief: Exploring Feelings, Loss and Death with Over Elevens and Adults* (2nd ed., 1993), Jessica Kingsley Publishers.

CHAPTER 7

Self-Esteem

Self-esteem is the overall sense of value, worth, and confidence that a person has in themselves. It involves how much they appreciate and like themselves, regardless of the circumstances. High self-esteem is characterized by positive feelings about oneself, a sense of competence, and a belief in one's ability to handle life's challenges. Low self-esteem, on the other hand, is marked by negative feelings about oneself, self-doubt, and a lack of confidence in one's abilities. Self-esteem is influenced by various factors, including personal experiences, relationships, and societal messages.

Many children suffer from a damaged sense of self. Some children have such profound self-esteem deficits that they have internalized the belief that they are bad and their future is hopeless. The goal of enhancing self-esteem for these children is not an easy one, yet it is an essential component of any successful treatment program. In order to help children achieve this important treatment goal, various games can be implemented from this chapter. These games can be used as tools to help children focus on their strengths and abilities, experience feelings of self-worth, accept imperfection, and develop a more optimistic attitude.

To be truly effective at strengthening a child's self-esteem, caregivers must be part of the process. Caregivers need to be taught and coached how to interact with their children in a positive way, as well as how to foster their children's unique talents. The games in this chapter are, therefore, greatly enhanced by working in conjunction with caregivers.

BRAVO BINGO*

Introduction

Self-esteem plays a crucial role in a child's emotional development and overall well-being, shaping how they view themselves and interact with the world. Bravo Bingo is a fun, engaging group activity designed to increase positive self-statements and boost self-esteem. Players create personalized bingo cards filled with affirmations, which they reflect on as they play. The activity encourages sharing, self-reflection, and group bonding in a supportive environment.

Goals

- Increase positive statements about self

Materials

- *Bravo Bingo* card and statements templates (provided)
- Paper or cardstock
- Scissors and glue (enough for all players)
- Small bag
- Bingo tokens
- Star stickers
- Small gift bag with a gift tag

Advance Preparation

- Copy one *Bravo Bingo Card* onto colored cardstock for each player. Copy one *Bravo Bingo Statements* sheet for each player, plus an additional one to cut into separate squares. Fold the cut-out statements and place them into a small bag for the bingo caller.
- Place the star stickers in the gift bag and write on the gift tag: "You are a superstar!"

Instructions

1. Give each player a *Bravo Bingo Card* and a *Bravo Bingo Statements* sheet. Each player chooses 24 of the 30 statements, cuts them out, and glues them, in any order, on their bingo card.

2. Lead the group in playing bingo as usual. When a player wins, they call out, "Bravo!" The winner takes the gift bag, reads the message aloud, and distributes the stickers to all players. Group members can share in what way they are a "superstar."

3. Ask process questions such as:
   - Choose one statement on your Bravo Bingo card and share how it applies to you.
   - How do you feel when you read positive statements about yourself?
   - What are some other qualities or strengths you are proud of that aren't on your card?
   - How can this activity help you think more positively about yourself in the future?

---

* Adapted from *Paper Dolls and Paper Airplanes: Therapeutic Exercises for Sexually Traumatized Children,* by G. Crisci, M. Lay, & L. Lowenstein (1998), Kidsrights.

BRAVO BINGO CARD

B	R	A	V	O
		FREE		

BRAVO BINGO STATEMENTS

I am kind	I am a good friend	I am a good listener	There are things I do well	I can be kind to myself
I am friendly	I can do hard things	I know how to play fair	I am learning to take care of myself	It's okay to feel all my feelings
I'm a hard worker	I can make good decisions	My body is precious	I can be a good friend to myself	I am courageous
I can feel proud of my accomplishments	I can do my best	I have a right to say no to unwanted touch	I keep trying even when it's hard	I am creative
I am loving	I can stand up for myself	I can think positive thoughts	I am a good person	I have a good sense of humor
I know nobody is perfect	There is nobody else exactly like me	All my feelings are okay	I am lovable	I can create my own future

COGNITIVE BEHAVIORAL
ANGRY BIRDS GAME*

AGES: 8+   **MODALITY:** INDIVIDUAL

Introduction

This activity uses the metaphor of the Angry Birds game to teach cognitive behavioral therapy (CBT) concepts by helping clients visualize and replace negative self-talk with positive self-statements. Through engaging gameplay, children can better understand and internalize these important cognitive processes in an interactive way.

Goals

- Replace negative self-talk with appropriate positive self-talk
- Increase positive self-statements

Materials

- Angry Birds: Knock on Wood game

Instructions

1. Provide some basic psychoeducation on how to identify one's negative, distorted self-talk and replace it with more positive, realistic self-talk. Give a few examples of each.

2. Explain: "We are going to build a tower and place the pigs on it. We will then use the angry birds to knock down the tower. The pigs represent negative self-talk and the angry birds stand for positive self-talk, or 'truth bombs.' You will build the first tower and I will knock it down. Next, I will build a tower that you get to knock down."

3. The client will begin by building a tower. They can use a game card as an example or create their own design. The tower needs at least one pig, which will represent a negative self-talk statement that the client identifies. You will then use the catapult to launch angry birds at the client's tower while offering positive replacement thoughts to defeat the pig.

4. Optional: If following the directions of the Angry Birds: Knock on Wood game, each card has a certain number of points that the player will get if the pigs are knocked down and bonus points for getting the star or the eggs. You can keep track of points if desired.

5. In each round of the game, choose new negative and positive self-talk statements. Alternate between the client being the tower builder and the one using the catapult.

6. Ask process questions such as:
   - How will you feel if you believe a negative self-talk statement?
   - How will you feel if you believe the positive self-talk statement?

---

* Intervention by Tasha Milligan, MA, LPC, RPT™

- How can asking yourself questions about your feelings help you better understand your self-talk?
- Are all thoughts that pop up in your head true? Why or why not?
- What would your friends say about your negative self-talk statement?
- What would your parents think about your negative self-talk statement?
- When did you first believe this self-talk statement?
- If another child says something mean about you, is it true?
- How can you be intentional about thinking the best about yourself and others?
- Have you ever believed something that was not true? How did it impact you?

EMPOWER

Introduction

This activity fosters self-esteem, teamwork, and creativity in children and adolescents by involving them in the creation of their own game board. Through this process, participants express individuality, collaborate, and take ownership of their experience. The activity integrates therapeutic elements such as sharing achievements, giving compliments, and practicing kindness. As participants advance in the game, they build self-awareness, emotional expression, and teamwork. The combination of personal empowerment and structured therapeutic goals creates a holistic experience that promotes both individual and group growth.

Goals

- Build self-awareness, emotional expression, and social skills
- Recognize and affirm personal strengths and achievements
- Develop cooperation and teamwork through a shared creation process

Materials

- *Empower Game Components* (provided)
- Large colored cardboard sheet
- Paper or cardstock
- Markers
- Scissors
- Glue
- Decorative craft supplies (stickers, glitter, etc.)
- Die or spinner
- Playing piece (such as a small figurine or object)

Advance Preparation

- Make at least one copy of the *Empower Game Components*. Note that the "Team Up" component involves a mystery challenge that you will pose to the players, so prepare any materials you might need for this. It could be a trivia question, a simple puzzle, the human knot challenge (if touch is appropriate), a riddle, or another cooperative task of your choosing.

Instructions

1. Explain the activity: The participants are empowered to work as a team to create their own custom board game focused on self-esteem. Encourage them to collaborate with each other and use their creativity to design their game. They will create a game board from the materials provided and can customize the gameplay rules however they wish, as long as they meet these requirements:

    - They must incorporate all of the *Empower Game Components* in some way (e.g., as game cards or spaces on the game board).

- All players must get at least one turn.
- There is one shared playing piece, and the players work together to move it from the starting point to the end of the board. Once the playing piece reaches the end, all players win together.

2. Encourage the participants to discuss and agree on additional aspects of the game, such as how the game will get started, bonus spaces, and additional rules.

3. Once the board is complete, have the participants play the game they have created.

4. Ask process questions such as:
   - How did it feel to work together on designing the game board?
   - What was your favorite part of creating and playing the game?
   - How can this activity help build your self-esteem?

EMPOWER GAME COMPONENTS

PROUD MOMENT

Share a personal achievement from the past year.

Act of Kindness

Re-enact a scene where you were kind to someone.

Compliment

Give a heartfelt compliment to the person on your left.

STRENGTH

Draw something that represents one of your personal strengths.

SELF-CARE

Act out a self-care activity while the other players guess what it is.

TEAM UP

Work with the other players to complete a fun group challenge.

Start ➡

Finish

FEEL-GOODS

AGES: 10+   **MODALITY:** INDIVIDUAL

Introduction

This engaging self-esteem-building activity is designed to encourage positive self-reflection and reinforce the use of affirming self-statements. Through a creative process involving unwrapping a gift, participants answer thought-provoking questions that guide them toward recognizing their strengths and positive qualities. The client creates a personalized frame filled with affirmations, which serves as a tangible reminder of their capabilities and self-worth.

Goals

- Increase the frequency of positive self-statements
- Articulate at least five personal strengths

Materials

- *Feel-Good Messages* (provided)
- Five sheets of wrapping or tissue paper (in two different colors)
- Colored cardstock
- Scissors
- Glue
- Wooden DIY picture frame kit
- Paint or colored markers
- Decorative craft supplies (e.g., rhinestones, glitter)

Advance Preparation

- Wrap the wooden picture frame in five layers of wrapping or tissue paper, alternating between two colors.
- Copy and cut out the *Feel-Good Messages*.
- Cut out the colored cardstock so it fits into the picture frame.

Instructions

1. Explain: "This game is designed to help you think positively about yourself. You'll answer some questions, and after each question is answered, you get to unwrap a layer of your gift. Once you've answered all the questions, you'll reach the final gift!"

2. Ask the client the following questions. After each question is answered, allow the client to unwrap one layer of the gift. Encourage reflection after each question to help them connect with their positive feelings.

   - What's something you can do to help yourself feel better?
   - Tell about a proud moment.
   - Tell about a time you were kind to someone.
   - Tell about a time you were kind to yourself.
   - Say something you feel grateful for.

3. Once all layers are unwrapped, the frame is revealed. Explain that this frame is special because it will hold positive messages they can read whenever they need a reminder of their strengths.

4. Present the *Feel-Good Messages* to the client. Ask them to choose the messages that resonate with them the most. Have them cut these messages out and glue them onto the precut cardstock.

5. The client can decorate the frame using the available supplies.

6. Encourage the client to take the frame home and place it somewhere they can see it every day. Explain that reading these positive messages can help boost their self-esteem and remind them of their strengths.

7. Ask process questions such as:

   - How did you feel after sharing your proud moment or kind action?
   - What thoughts or feelings come up when you think about being kind to yourself?
   - How do you think practicing self-kindness can help you in difficult situations?
   - How can this frame of positive affirmations help you?

There are things I can do to help myself feel better.

I can feel good about my proud moments.

I know it's okay to make mistakes.

BEING KIND TO OTHERS MAKES ME FEEL GOOD ABOUT MYSELF.

When I think positive thoughts, it makes me feel better.

I FEEL PROUD OF MYSELF WHEN I TRY MY BEST.

I MAY FAIL, BUT I CAN TRY AGAIN.

I AM A FIGHTER WHO DOES NOT GIVE UP.

I am capable of doing hard things.

I can be kind to myself.

I can ask for help when I need it.

I can make a difference in the world.

I AM LOVED.

I can be happy for all that I have.

FEELING POSITIVE EVERY DAY*

Introduction

This activity is designed to help children explore and strengthen their self-esteem. Through an interactive game format, players reflect on their positive traits, share compliments, and reinforce healthy self-statements. The goal is to cultivate a positive mindset and enhance self-awareness in a supportive group setting.

Goals

- Define self-esteem
- Increase the frequency of positive self-statements

Materials

- Game board (provided)
- Colored cardstock or paper
- 34 index cards
- Marker
- Happy face stickers (one per player)
- Star stickers (one per player)
- Hershey's Kisses (one per player)

Advance Preparation

- Copy the game board onto colored cardstock or paper. (Optional: Make one copy per client for them to take home.)
- Number the index cards from 1 to 31 (write the number large in the center of the card). The remaining three cards are used for "surprise" game cards. Write one of the following statements on each of the surprise cards:
  - "You have a nice smile! Take a happy face sticker and give one to each player who shows you their nice smile."
  - "You are special! Take a Hershey's Kiss and give one to each player."
  - "You are a superstar! Take a star sticker and give one to each player."
- Arrange the cards so they are not in order and intersperse the "surprise" cards among the deck.

Instructions

1. Have the players sit in a circle with the game board in the middle. Place the game cards face down beside the game board.

2. Define self-esteem. For example, say, "Self-esteem is how we feel about ourselves. It's like having an inner voice that tells us whether we are good, important, and capable of doing

---

* Adapted from *Paper Dolls and Paper Airplanes: Therapeutic Exercises for Sexually Traumatized Children,* by G. Crisci, M. Lay, & L. Lowenstein (1998), Kidsrights.

things. When we have healthy self-esteem, we believe in ourselves and feel proud of who we are!"

3. Explain: "We are going to play a game about self-esteem. We will take turns picking the game card at the top of the pile. The number on the card corresponds with a question on the game board for the player to read aloud and answer. There are three surprise cards in the deck. The game is finished once all the cards have been used. In this game, there are no losers—only winners!"

4. Ask process questions such as:
   - How did it feel to give or receive a compliment during the game?
   - What did you learn about yourself while playing this game?
   - Which question was the hardest for you to answer? Why?
   - How can you use the ideas from this game in your daily life to boost your self-esteem?

5. Optional: Give each client a copy of the game board to take home. Encourage them to read one prompt each day and reflect on it, journal or draw about it, or share about it with their caregiver.

FEELING POSITIVE EVERY DAY: GAME BOARD

Monday	Tuesday	Wednesday	Thursday	Friday	Saturday	Sunday
1 Define self-esteem.	2 Name something you like about yourself.	3 Tell about a time when you felt proud of yourself.	4 Give a compliment to the person on your left.	5 What's one thing that cheers you up?	6 Tell about something you have done well recently.	7 What can you do to feel better when you're upset?
8 Tell about something nice someone did for you.	9 What's something you enjoy doing at school?	10 What do you like best about yourself?	11 Tell about a time when you felt smart.	12 What is the bravest thing you ever did?	13 True or false: There's no such thing as a perfect person.	14 What is something you do better than most people?
15 What's something you enjoy doing at home?	16 What's something you need when you're upset?	17 Tell about a happy moment in your life.	18 Who can you talk to when you're upset?	19 Say something that's special about you.	20 What's something about yourself that you have the power to change?	21 Tell about something that makes you feel good.
22 What's something you can tell yourself when you're upset?	23 Give a compliment to the person on your right.	24 Name something that makes you laugh.	25 What would a friend say they like about you?	26 Tell about a time when you did something difficult.	27 Tell about something nice you did for someone.	28 Next time you are upset, what can you do to feel better?
29 What is a respectful way to stand up to a bully?	30 Tell about a time when you felt special.	31 What's something you're looking forward to?				

HIGHS AND LOWS

AGES: 10+   **MODALITY:** INDIVIDUAL

Introduction

Building self-esteem in children is crucial for fostering emotional resilience and a positive self-concept. This game encourages reflection on both positive and negative self-talk, which can be an effective tool for helping children understand and improve their self-esteem.

Goals

- Verbalize an understanding of self-esteem
- Increase positive self-statements

Materials

- *Highs and Lows Questions* (provided)
- Standard 52-card deck
- Small, inexpensive prizes

Instructions

1. Explain: "Self-esteem is how we feel about ourselves most of the time. High self-esteem means we feel positive about ourselves, our abilities, and our choices much of the time. Low self-esteem means we struggle to see the good in ourselves, we have negative thoughts about ourselves, and we doubt our abilities. This game will help you learn about self-esteem as well as how to turn negative self-talk into positive self-talk."

2. Shuffle the deck of cards. Without looking at the cards, randomly pick 20. Lay these 20 cards in a row face down. You could also have the client do this part (self-esteem builder!).

3. Turn over the first card in the row. The client guesses whether the next card is higher or lower than the first to earn a point. (Aces count as 1; royalty cards are 10.)

4. If the next card is higher than the first, choose a question from the "Highs" list for the client to answer. If the card is lower, choose a question from the "Lows" list for them to answer. With the "Lows" prompts, keep the client focused on simply identifying (or even challenging) their negative self-talk; you do not want to unintentionally encourage rumination.

5. Play until all the cards have been turned over. At the end of the game, trade points for prizes: 1–15 points = 1 prize, 16 or more points = 2 prizes.

6. Ask process questions such as:
   - How did you feel when you talked about your "lows"? What about when you shared your "highs"?
   - How do you think positive self-talk can help when you're feeling upset?
   - Can you think of a time when you turned a bad day around by focusing on something good?

HIGHS AND LOWS

Highs	Lows
• Imagine you do well on a test. Say something positive to yourself. • Say something you feel grateful for. • Say something you like about your appearance. • Tell about a time someone gave you a compliment. • Tell about a proud moment. • Imagine you drop something special and it breaks. Turn a negative self-statement into a positive self-statement. • Tell about a joyful moment. • Tell about a time you were kind to someone. • Tell about a time someone did something kind for you. • Imagine you mess up while playing a video game. Turn a negative self-statement into a positive self-statement. • Tell about a time you were able to do something difficult. • Imagine you didn't study for a test and you get a bad grade. Turn a negative self-statement into a positive self-statement. • Imagine you didn't get invited to a classmate's birthday party. Turn a negative self-statement into a positive self-statement. • Tell about a time you tried your best, regardless of the outcome. • Tell about a time you used a healthy coping strategy.	• Tell about a time you failed or did poorly at something. What negative thoughts did you have about yourself? • Say something you wish was different about your life. • Say something you wish you could change about your appearance. • Tell about a time someone said something hurtful to you. • Tell about a time you were teased or felt excluded. • Tell about a time someone disappointed you. • Imagine you drop something special and it breaks. What negative self-talk might pop up in your head in that situation? • Tell about a time you felt jealous. • Tell about a time you made a mistake. • Tell about a time you were unkind to someone. • Imagine you mess up while playing a video game. What negative self-talk might pop up in your head? • Tell about a time when things didn't go as planned. • Tell about a time you felt frustrated. • Imagine you didn't study for a test and you get a bad grade. What negative self-talk might pop up in your head? • Imagine you didn't get invited to a classmate's birthday party. What negative self-talk might pop up in your head?

SELF-ESTEEM SEARCH PARTY

AGES: 12+   **MODALITY:** INDIVIDUAL

Introduction

This activity aims to help teens explore and enhance their self-esteem through social media and online resources. Participants will use prompts and dice to guide their search for positive and affirming content on the internet. This interactive approach encourages teens to reflect on self-esteem concepts while utilizing familiar platforms.

Goals

- Verbalize an understanding of the importance of self-esteem
- Increase positive self-statements

Materials

- Prompts list (provided)
- Computer or other device with internet access
- Two standard dice
- Paper and writing utensils

Instructions

1. Explain: "We will play five rounds of this game. At the beginning of each round, we will both write down a number from 1 to 12. We will take turns rolling the dice. The winner of the round is the player whose number is closest to the number rolled. The winner chooses one of the prompts from the list, and chooses whether they or their opponent finds the answer to the prompts by searching online."

2. Ask process questions such as:
   - Which prompt was your favorite and why?
   - Name something you learned about self-esteem.
   - How did the content you found make you feel about yourself? Why?
   - Which type of prompt (e.g., video, quote, image) did you find most impactful, and how can you use it in your daily life?
   - What new strategies or tools for improving self-esteem will you try based on what you discovered during the activity?

SELF-ESTEEM SEARCH PARTY: PROMPTS

- Definition of self-esteem

- Example of positive self-talk

- Positive affirmation

- Poem about healthy self-esteem

- Advertisement that promotes a positive body image

- Video about healthy self-esteem

- Meme about healthy self-esteem

- Social media influencer who promotes healthy self-esteem

- Motivational quote

- Song lyrics that promote positive self-esteem

- An article about an act of kindness

- Something you would put on your vision board

- Image that portrays something you feel grateful for

- Image that portrays a personal achievement

SMILEY FACES*

AGES: 7–12 **MODALITY:** INDIVIDUAL, GROUP, FAMILY

Introduction

This game helps children internalize positive thoughts to enhance self-esteem. It helps children realize that they have the power to change how they feel by reframing their negative thoughts and focusing on positive things.

Goals

- Increase positive self-statements
- Reframe negative thoughts into positive ones

Materials

- *Smiley Faces* game board (provided)
- One pawn
- One standard die
- Gift bag filled with inexpensive items, preferably with smiley faces
- Bright yellow cardboard or poster board, black marker, scissors, and tape (optional)

Advance Preparation

- Photocopy and enlarge the *Smiley Faces* game. If possible, laminate it onto cardboard for greater durability.
- Optional: Cut the yellow cardboard into circles the size of a paper plate, one for each person in the group. Use a black marker to draw a happy face on each circle.

Instructions

1. Explain that people generally feel happier if they have a positive attitude, focus on happy thoughts, and do things that make them feel good. Explain that the purpose of this game is to help each person develop a more positive attitude so that they can feel better.

2. Players sit in a circle with the game board in the middle of the circle. Place the pawn on the last space (question 10).

3. Players take turns rolling the die. An even number means advance the pawn to the next space on the board and answer the question written on it. An odd number means the pawn doesn't move. When a player lands on a space that has a happy face, distribute items from the gift bag to everyone in the group.

4. Play until the pawn reaches the final happy face (after all the questions have been answered).

---

* Adapted from *Creative Interventions for Troubled Children and Youth,* by L. Lowenstein (1999), Champion Press.

5. For a closing activity after the game, tape the precut cardboard happy faces to the backs of each group member (including yourself), and have everyone write something nice on each other's happy faces. This is a nice memento for each person to take home.

6. Ask process questions such as:
   - How do you feel when you focus on positive thoughts?
   - How do you think having a positive attitude can help you in everyday life?
   - What was your favorite part of the game?

SMILEY FACES GAME BOARD

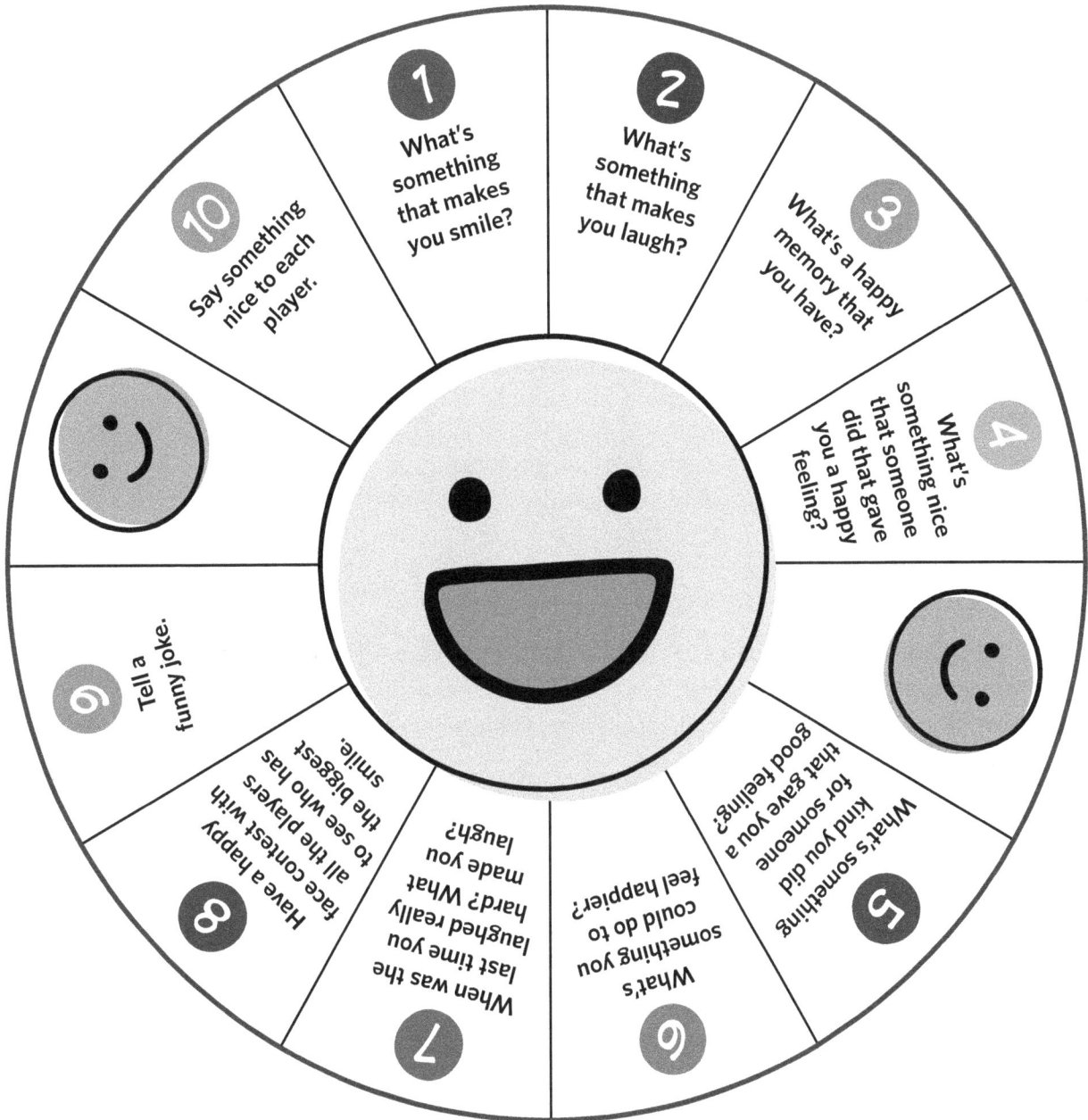

1. What's something that makes you smile?

2. What's something that makes you laugh?

3. What's a happy memory that you have?

4. What's something nice that someone did that gave you a happy feeling?

5. What's something kind you did for someone that gave you a good feeling?

6. What's something you could do to feel happier?

7. When was the last time you laughed really hard? What made you laugh?

8. Have a happy face contest with all the players to see who has the biggest smile.

9. Tell a funny joke.

10. Say something nice to each player.

STRENGTHS STORY

AGES: 8+   **MODALITY:** INDIVIDUAL, GROUP, FAMILY

Introduction

In this activity, children will engage in a collaborative storytelling game designed to highlight strengths, positive experiences, and challenges they have overcome. Using game cards, they will build a story about a character who faces a challenge and overcomes it using their strengths. This activity encourages creativity and reflection on personal growth, helping children recognize their own resilience.

Goals

- Identify personal strengths clients have used to overcome real-life challenges
- Increase positive self-statements

Materials

- Cardstock or paper, preferably in five different colors
- Scissors
- Coloring utensils

Advance Preparation

- Cut the cardstock into squares to create a set of game cards. The cards should include the following categories, with five to six cards in each category. Write the category number and name at the top of each card and, ideally, use a different color of cardstock for each category:

  1. **Positive Trait** (e.g., courageous, kind, creative)

  2. **Challenge** (e.g., being bullied, making a mistake, feeling anxious)

  3. **Positive Action** (e.g., being assertive, helping others, talking about feelings)

  4. **Positive Emotion** (e.g., proud, brave, confident)

  5. **Triumphant Object** (e.g., trophy, star, high five)

Instructions

1. Place the game cards face up on a table or the floor. The cards serve as prompts to guide participants in building a story based on their own (or aspirational) strengths, positive experiences, and challenges they've overcome.

2. The first participant begins the story by introducing a main character who is their age. They choose a Positive Trait card (e.g., courageous) and begin the story: "This is a story about a courageous 10-year-old named Sammy."

3. The next participant continues the story by adding a Challenge faced by the main character: "One day, Sammy was at recess, and a group of kids started to bully Sammy."

4. The next participant chooses a Positive Action for the main character to perform: "Sammy decided to be assertive. Sammy told the bullies to stop being mean."

5. The next participant chooses a Positive Emotion that relates to the story: "Sammy felt proud for standing up to the bullies."

6. The next participant chooses a Triumphant Object and continues the story: "Another kid who had been bullied saw Sammy stand up to the bullies, so they gave Sammy a high five!"

7. Encourage the clients to reflect on how the character's strengths help them overcome difficulties or how they grow from challenges. Ask process questions such as:
   - How did the character's strengths help them face the challenge?
   - What emotions did the character feel during the story, and why?
   - What was the most important action the character took, and how did it change the outcome?
   - How can you relate the character's experience to your own life?

CHAPTER 8

Family Interaction and Attachment

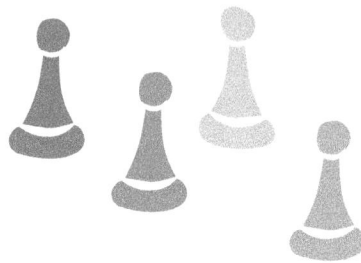

In this chapter, the focus is on using therapeutic games as tools to foster communication and emotional connection among family members. The games presented are designed to help families communicate more openly and effectively, allowing them to express their thoughts and feelings in a safe and supportive environment. Through these interventions, family members develop empathy and come to better understand each other's perspectives. Additionally, these games provide opportunities to strengthen parenting skills, which in turn supports a healthier parent-child relationship.

Incorporating family games into sessions adds another layer of benefit to play therapy. Family play therapy allows both children and parents to engage in meaningful interactions that help build trust and emotional security. Games, in particular, offer a fun, low-pressure way for family members to work through conflicts, share experiences, and build stronger bonds. By participating in therapeutic games, families can develop healthier patterns of communication and cooperation, which ultimately leads to positive and lasting changes in their relationships.

COOPERATION AND COMPLIMENTS

Introduction

This activity is designed to enhance family cooperation and positive interaction by incorporating engaging games that require teamwork among siblings. By focusing on the use of labeled praise, it helps caregivers consistently reinforce and encourage their children's positive behaviors, fostering a more supportive and harmonious family environment.

Goals

- Improve positive interaction within the family
- Encourage the caregiver to consistently praise the children

Materials

- *Cooperation and Compliments Games* cards (provided)
- Balloon
- Paper
- Pen
- Standard 52-card deck
- Scissors
- Straws
- Paper plates
- Timer
- Small notebook

Advance Preparation

- Prior to the family session, be sure the caregiver understands the concept of labeled praise (telling your child exactly what they are doing that you like).
- Copy the game description cards and cut them out.

Instructions

1. Explain the activity to the children: "You will take turns choosing games to play from these cards. These are cooperative games, so you must work together. Your parent will cheer you on and give compliments when you cooperate well together."

2. The caregiver's role during the session is to focus on the children's positive behavior by using labeled praise (e.g., "Great job working together to keep the balloon in the air," "Wow, you both did such an amazing job balancing that," "I like the way you took turns being the leader").

3. Ask the caregiver process questions such as:
   - How did using labeled praise during the game change your perception of your children's interactions? Can you share a specific moment that stood out to you?
   - In what ways did you notice your children cooperating more effectively during the game? How do you think your compliments influenced this behavior?
   - How can you incorporate labeled praise into daily routines to encourage positive behavior and cooperation between your children?

4. Ask the children process questions such as:

   - How did working together with your sibling during the game make you feel? Can you give an example of a time you cooperated well?

   - What was the best part of receiving compliments from your parent while you played the games? How did it affect how you worked with your sibling?

   - Can you think of other activities at home where you can work together and support each other like you did in the game?

5. Provide the caregiver with a small notebook to take home. Encourage the caregiver to write in the notebook at least one labeled praise statement about each child every day at bedtime, and to read this labeled praise statement aloud to the child. Emphasize that spending two minutes per day doing this will lead to improved behavior and a more positive environment within the family. Give examples of labeled praise statements:

   - I appreciate the effort you put into [*e.g., cleaning your room*].

   - I'm proud of you for [*playing so nicely with your brother*].

   - I like the way you [*asked nicely for a treat*].

   - Thank you for [*brushing your teeth when I asked you to*].

   - You [*calmed yourself when you felt angry*]. Way to go!

   - You are so [*creative*]! I love playing with you.

COOPERATION AND COMPLIMENTS GAMES

Balloon Carry: Work together to carry a balloon between your bodies without using your hands. You must carry the balloon to the other end of the room. If the balloon drops, you must start over.

Balloon Bounce: Work together to keep the balloon from hitting the ground. Time it, then do it again to try to beat your record.

Balance the Object: Place a pen on a sheet of paper. You must each hold a different end of the paper. Try to balance the pen on the paper while walking from one end of the room to the other. If the pen falls off, you must start over.

Quick Cards: Shuffle a deck of cards. Work together to put the cards in order, starting with red cards from ace to king, then black cards from ace to king. Time it, then do it again and try to break your record.

Suck It Up: Cut a sheet of paper into 30 small squares and crumple them up. Put the clumps on a paper plate and place a second paper plate beside it. Set a timer for one minute. Put straws in your mouths and use suction to move the paper clumps from one plate to another. If a clump falls along the way, it is put back onto the first plate. See how many clumps you can transfer in one minute. Then repeat and try to break your record.

Mirror Walk: Walk from one end of the room to the other. One of you leads by walking in a certain way (such as stomping like a dinosaur) and the other must follow closely, mirroring the first person's movements exactly. Then switch roles.

FAMILY AVATAR QUEST*

AGES: 8+   **MODALITY:** FAMILY

Introduction

This game is designed to promote perspective taking and enhance family collaboration by engaging participants in a creative and interactive activity. By working together to create a unique avatar and discussing their choices, family members deepen their understanding of each other's viewpoints and values, fostering stronger connections and open communication.

Goals

- Promote perspective taking
- Increase open communication and collaboration within the family
- Deepen family members' understanding of each other to build stronger connections

Materials

- Computer or other device with internet access
- Digital avatar creation interface (e.g., https://readyplayer.me/avatar)
- Virtual dice (e.g., https://toytheater.com/dice/)

Instructions

1. Each family member rolls a die to determine the order of play (from the player with the highest number through the player with the lowest number). In case of a tie, the players who rolled the same number will roll again to determine which of the two goes before the other.

2. The family members takes turns adding a component of their choice to the avatar (e.g., facial features, hairstyle, outfit, accessories, background story). Changes to each component can only be made by the player who initially chose that characteristic; players cannot change another player's selection.

3. After each addition, give the family a discussion prompt to encourage perspective taking and communication. You can use the following questions or create your own to align with the family's therapeutic goals:

   - **Appearance:** What made you choose this [*e.g., hairstyle, clothing*] for the avatar? How does it influence your thoughts and feelings about the avatar? How do you think it impacts how others perceive the avatar?

   - **Background:** What family structure or traits did you choose for the avatar? How might this influence their behavior and perspective? How does the avatar's background affect their habits, traditions, and values?

   - **Personality:** What personality traits did you select for the avatar? How do these traits influence their view of themselves, others' views of them, and their interactions?

---

* Intervention by Rachel Altvater, PsyD, RPT-S™

What hobby or interest did you give the avatar? How might this shape their social circle and experiences?

4. After the family has finalized their avatar, prompt them to reflect on the process, explore how the avatar's characteristics connect to real-life perspectives, and deepen mutual understanding among the family members. You can ask reflection questions such as:

- How did it feel to make decisions about the avatar as a family?
- What did you learn about each other's perspectives?
- How do you think the avatar would navigate a difficult situation? How might each family member's contribution influence this?
- Discuss how each family member's contributions to the avatar reflect their own values and interests.
- Describe a moment during the game that was particularly meaningful to you.

FAMILY COMMUNICATION WITH MINIATURE FIGURINES*

AGES: 8+   **MODALITY:** FAMILY

Introduction

This activity is intended to help families explore communication issues and learn how their communication impacts each other. In this game, the family uses miniature figurines to communicate without the use of nonverbal communication in order to better understand its impact.

Goals

- Learn, practice, and implement appropriate communication skills
- Learn about nonverbal communication and its impact on interactions
- Verbally express a range of emotions

Materials

- Miniature figurines

Instructions

1. Begin by asking the family what it means to communicate. Discuss what verbal communication is (talking, responding) and what nonverbal communication looks like (sighs, eye rolls, shoulder shrugs, turning away, etc.). Ask the family to use their bodies and facial expressions to show examples of nonverbal communication. Discuss examples of nonverbal communication that may lead to upset (e.g., child rolls their eyes when asked to clean their room).

2. Explain the game:
   - This activity will help you improve your communication and discuss topics more freely without the impact of nonverbal factors. We will practice speaking without seeing each other so we do not have body language and facial expressions causing negative reactions to topics.
   - To play this game, each of you will pick a miniature that represents a happy family memory. The trick to this game is to not show each other your miniatures, and you will sit back to back when you play. One person will start as the speaker and one person with start as the listener. You will take turns describing your miniature and talking about why you picked it. After the speaker describes their miniature, the listener must repeat back what they heard.
   - I will continue to guide you through these steps as we go. At the end of this activity, you can guess what miniature your family member picked!

---

* Intervention by Katie Musa, PhD, IMFT-S, LPCC-S, RPT™. Adapted from "I Said, You Said: A Communication Exercise for Couples," by P. Parr, R. A. Boyle, & L. Tejada, 2008, *Contemporary Family Therapy, 30,* pp. 167–173 (https://doi.org/10.1007/s10591-008-9062-6).

3. Prompt the listener to repeat back what they heard, and have the speaker correct the listener if needed.

4. Play several rounds, first asking the family members to pick miniatures that represent happy memories together, and then asking them to choose miniatures that represent more complex issues, such as sad memories or times someone in the family made them angry.

5. Ask process questions such as:

   - What was it like not seeing each other while you spoke to each other?
   - What was it like being in the role of the speaker and the role of the listener?
   - How might you use an exercise like this at home?

FAMILY TREE IN MINECRAFT*

Introduction

In this activity, families engage in a creative exploration of their relationships and identities using the Minecraft video game. Participants symbolically represent themselves and other family members by choosing and placing items on a shared "family tree" within the game world. This process encourages emotional expression, self-awareness, and open communication, allowing family members to gain insight into their relational dynamics in a playful and interactive setting.

> **Note:** This intervention is for use with children who are familiar with and enjoy using the Minecraft video game. Therapists must be appropriately trained in the use of Minecraft in clinical settings. Using Minecraft as a therapeutic tool is not an official Minecraft product or service, nor is it approved by or associated with Mojang or Microsoft.

Goals

- Increase self-awareness and emotional expression
- Increase open communication and reflection among family members
- Develop insight into family dynamics and relational patterns

Materials

- Minecraft licenses for each player
- Computer, games console, or other device with internet access

Advance Preparation

- Watch the video guide for this activity (available at https://www.elliefinch.co.uk/activities).

Instructions

1. Explain the purpose of the activity: To explore family relationships, personal identity, and emotional expression using Minecraft. Encourage a comfortable and open atmosphere, where there is no "right" or "wrong" choice.

2. Instruct the family to find or grow a tree within the Minecraft world. Explain that this tree will represent their "family tree" and will be used to place symbolic items. Each participant will select an item from their inventory to represent themselves and place it on the tree. They can then select items that symbolize other family members (including pets or friends) as well.

3. Allow time for each participant to explain why they chose their specific item and where they placed it on the tree.

---

* Intervention by Ellie Finch, MA, MBACP (Accred.)

4. Encourage dialogue between family members to reflect on their choices. This can lead to discussions about how they see each other, any surprises in the choices, and how this symbolic representation connects to real-life dynamics.

5. Ask process questions such as:
   - How do you feel about the items chosen?
   - Did any of the item choices surprise you?
   - Would you change any of the choices?
   - What would need to happen in your family for the placement of these items to change?

6. Close the session by summarizing key insights or emotions that surfaced during the discussion. Allow each family member to reflect on any changes in understanding about themselves or their relationships that may have emerged through the activity.

7. Consider revisiting the tree in future sessions to reflect on progress or changes in family dynamics.

NATURE'S TREASURES TIC-TAC-TOE*

AGES: 6+   **MODALITY:** FAMILY

Introduction

This engaging family activity is designed to strengthen the parent-child relationship while encouraging outdoor exploration. It supports mindfulness and nature appreciation, while fostering teamwork and shared experiences in a safe outdoor space. Families can also enhance their learning by using a nature identification app as part of the experience.

Goals

- Strengthen the parent-child relationship
- Engage in a mindfulness-based activity
- Encourage the family to spend time together in nature

Materials

- Access to a safe, natural, outdoor space
- Seek by iNaturalist app (optional)

Advance Preparation

- Create a list of nature-based objects for the family to find outdoors. Ensure that some of the items can be used to create a tic-tac-toe game board (e.g., 4 long sticks, 5 small rocks, 5 small leaves, 5 blades of grass, a flower, something that is multicolored, something smaller than your thumb, something fuzzy, something smooth).

Instructions

1. Explain the game to the family: "This activity will help you all have fun together and learn something about nature. First, you will be going on a scavenger hunt outside together."

2. Accompany the family to a safe, natural space such as a park. Once outdoors, provide the family with your scavenger hunt list and ask them to find as many items on the list as they can.

3. Promote family connection by encouraging them to work together to find the items on the list. Prompt the parents to crouch down to the child's level or to hold the child's hand while they search for items.

4. During the scavenger hunt, facilitate mindfulness using prompts such as:
   - What do you see? Notice the colors. Are they bright or dull? Look very carefully and describe what you see in detail. Look for things that you have never noticed before.
   - What do you hear? How many different sounds do you hear? What are they? Where are they coming from? Are they loud or quiet? Pleasant or unpleasant?

---

* Intervention by Kathy Eugster, MA, RCC, CPT-S

- Feel the air on your skin. Is it cool or warm? Does it feel good or not so good? Do you notice anything else on your skin, like sunshine, raindrops, or wind?
- What can you smell? When you notice a smell, can you tell where the smell comes from? Are they pleasant or unpleasant smells?
- Notice your feet walking on the ground. Notice what it feels like to walk on different surfaces.

5. After the scavenger hunt, ask process questions such as:
   - Which item were you most excited to find?
   - Which item was the hardest to find?
   - What surprised you the most?
   - What are some other ways you can enjoy nature together as a family?
   - What other games might you enjoy playing together?

6. Once the family has found the items on the list (or after a preallotted time is up), invite the family to create a tic-tac-toe board and play the game using nature items found during the scavenger hunt.

7. Optional: Use the Seek by iNaturalist app (https://www.inaturalist.org/pages/seek_app) to identify plants and animals. By taking a picture of a living organism using the Seek app, one can learn about the plant or animal. The free Merlin Bird ID app (https://merlin.allaboutbirds.org) identifies any singing bird.

PAPARAZZI*

Introduction

This intervention helps families explore and understand each other's perceptions of family dynamics by taking on the role of paparazzi and capturing significant moments. By encouraging open communication and mutual understanding through drawing and discussion, this activity aims to strengthen family bonds and improve interactions.

Goals

- Explore each family member's perception of family dynamics
- Increase open communication in the family
- Facilitate mutual understanding

Materials

- Toy camera
- Paper and coloring utensils
- Standard 52-card deck

Instructions

1. Explain to the family that they are going to pretend to be paparazzi (people who take candid photos of celebrities). They will choose who will be the first paparazzo. This role will be rotated among family members during the game. The rest of the family can act normally or do a specific activity that everyone agrees on, such as playing cards or drawing together.

2. The paparazzo on duty must observe the family and take imaginary photos of moments that they consider important or interesting. After a few minutes, give a signal, and the role of paparazzo will change to another family member.

3. After everyone has had their turn as the paparazzo, distribute paper and coloring utensils to everyone. Each family member must draw their favorite "photograph" they took while they were the paparazzo, depicting the family members and their interactions.

4. Once everyone has finished their drawings, each family member presents their "photograph" and describes the moment, including the actions and emotions they observed.

5. Facilitate discussion with questions such as "What moment did you capture here?" "What do you think your family members are feeling in this moment?" and "Why did you choose that moment to photograph?"

---

* Intervention by Arlen Sarabia, PhD

6. Encourage the family to discuss different perceptions of each member and how they felt about being paparazzi and being photographed. Explore emotions and family dynamics that emerge from the drawings and conversations.

7. Ask process questions such as:
   - How did it feel to be both the paparazzo and the subject in the photographs? Did these roles change your perspective on your family members or yourself?
   - What did you learn about your family members from the moments they chose to "photograph"? Did any of the chosen moments surprise you? Why or why not?
   - Were there any moments you observed that made you feel uncomfortable or confused? How did you handle those feelings during the exercise?
   - How can the insights gained from this activity help improve communication and understanding within your family? What steps can you take moving forward to strengthen these dynamics?

8. In subsequent sessions, work with the family to develop strategies that improve family interaction and dynamics, based on the information and reflections obtained from this game.

PHOTOGRAPHS AND MEMORIES*

AGES: 7+   **MODALITY:** FAMILY

Introduction

This activity is designed to help families strengthen their bond by reflecting on shared memories through photographs and prompts. By engaging in a creative discussion of past experiences, children and caregivers can deepen their connection, foster positive communication, and preserve meaningful moments. It's a fun, interactive way to explore family history while building emotional attachment.

Goals

- Discuss and preserve positive family memories
- Strengthen family attachment

Materials

- *Caregiver Instructions* (provided)
- *Memory Cards* (provided)
- Paper or cardstock
- Scissors
- One standard die
- Writing or coloring utensils
- Stapler

Advance Preparation

- Copy the memory cards onto colored cardstock and cut them out.
- Give the caregiver the provided instructions so they can prepare the photos to bring to the session.
- Discuss with the caregiver appropriate things to say to their child during the session when they look at the photos together (e.g., "The day you were born was the happiest moment in my life," "You look so adorable in this picture!" "This photo shows your beautiful smile!").

Instructions

1. Lay all the photos and memory cards face up on the floor.

2. The child rolls the die. If they roll an even number (2, 4, 6), they choose one of the photos laid out on the floor to talk about with their caregiver. If they roll an odd number (1, 3, 5), they choose a memory card and provide an answer. The caregiver writes the child's answer on the memory card. Play until there are no photos or cards left.

3. At the end, compile a memory book with the photos and cards by stapling the pages together.

4. Ask process questions such as:
   - Point to your favorite photo in the memory book and say why it's your favorite.
   - What's something new you learned about your family from these photos?
   - How do you think your family has changed or grown over time?

---

* Adapted from *Cory Helps Kids Cope with Grief: Playful Activities for Young Children,* by L. Lowenstein (2024), Champion Press.

CAREGIVER INSTRUCTIONS: "PHOTOGRAPHS AND MEMORIES" ACTIVITY

For this activity, please prepare some family photos as described below and bring them with you to the therapy session. Each photo should be printed and taped to a sheet of paper. Write a caption under each photo that includes the date and a short description. If you do not have a photo of some of the suggested items, you can take photos of items around your home and community.

Suggested Photos

- Your child's baby picture

- 2-4 photos that depict family outings or vacations

- 2-3 photos of your child's birthday celebrations

- 2-3 photos that depict school events or your child's performances

- 2-3 photos that depict your child's important milestones

- A time your child did something funny

- A cute photo of your child

- Your child's favorite item at home

- Something your child made for you that you cherish

- Something that represents your family's culture

- 2-3 photos of extended family

MEMORY CARDS

A fun family memory:

Something nice someone in my family did for me:

A time someone in my family made me laugh:

A place where my family went that I liked:

Something that I am proud of that my family knows about:

A time my family celebrated something together:

A family tradition that I enjoy:

My favorite family meal:

Someone in my family who I admire:

Something that I love about my family:

TEEN TALK

Introduction

This activity fosters meaningful conversations between a teen and their parent. It encourages open communication, empathy, and positive interactions in a safe, structured environment. This activity is suitable for families who have established a basic level of trust and are ready to explore emotional topics together.

Goals

- Increase open communication within the family
- Increase the parent's empathy toward their child by remembering what it was like for them as a teen
- Increase the frequency of positive interactions between the parent and teen

Materials

- Question sheet (provided)
- Standard 52-card deck

Advance Preparation

- Photocopy the provided question sheet. Adapt the questions as needed so they are appropriate to the family.
- Meet with the parent prior to the session to explain the activity and its purpose. Encourage the parent to be appropriately open with their child about their life as a teen. Discuss specific examples of ways the parent can respond to the questions. Coach the parent to say at the beginning of the session with their teen: "It's okay to be open and honest. I won't be angry with you about anything you say."

Instructions

1. Divide the deck of cards evenly between the parent and teen.

2. Explain: "Each of you will flip over the top card from your deck at the same time. The player with the higher number gets to ask the other a question from the list, in order. Aces count as 1, and royalty cards count as 10. If you both get the same number, give each other a fist bump, then flip over the next card. If the person being asked the question does not want to answer, they can pass. I might ask the person answering the question to elaborate. We will play until all questions have been answered."

3. Ask the parent process questions such as:
   - What is different about your child's teen years and yours?
   - What did this activity make you realize about your life as a teen? About your child's life?
   - What similarities are there between what your life was like as a teen and your child's life?

4. Ask the teen process questions such as:
   - What did you learn about your parent's life that you didn't know before?
   - How was your parent's childhood similar to or different from yours?
   - Did anything you learned today about your parent surprise you? If so, what?
   - Are there any connections between what your parent was like as a teen and the problems your family is getting help with today?

5. To close the activity, consider a joint reflection where the parent and teen express gratitude for each other's openness and courage.

TEEN TALK QUESTIONS

For the teen to ask their parent:

- When you were a teen, what was one of your favorite things to do?

- When you were a teen, who was a musician or band that you liked?

- When you were a teen, what was a rule in your home that you hated?

- When you were a teen, what was something you did that you now regret?

- When you were a teen, what worried you?

- When you were a teen, what's something your parent did that really upset you?

- When you were a teen, what was something you accomplished that made you feel proud?

For the parent to ask their teen:

- What is one of the funnest things you ever did?

- What is one of your favorite songs and why?

- What is a rule in our home that you hate?

- What is something you did that you now regret?

- What is something that worries you?

- What is something that I do that really upsets you?

- What is something you have accomplished that makes you feel proud?

TOSS THE BALL*

Introduction

This is a family-based game designed to foster open communication, strengthen family bonds, and assess family dynamics in a playful and interactive manner. By engaging in a series of ball-tossing rounds where participants share affirmations, wishes, and areas for personal growth, family members can build a deeper understanding of each other while creating a collaborative environment for positive change.

Goals

- Increase playful interaction within the family
- Increase open communication among family members
- Assess family relationships and dynamics
- Identify areas for change within the family

Materials

- Soft ball that can be easily and safely tossed
- Timer

Instructions

1. Explain that the family members will take turns gently tossing the ball to each other. As they toss the ball to someone, they are to say something nice to that family member. The pattern is repeated for five minutes or until every person has heard at least two nice things about themselves.

2. Ask each person to describe their experience. For example:
   - What was it like to say nice things to everyone?
   - How did you feel when another member of your family said something nice to you?
   - Did you receive any unexpected comments?

3. After processing, start the game again; however, this time ask them to tell something they would enjoy doing (but are not currently doing) with the person to whom they throw the ball. This continues until every person has tossed the ball to each family member.

---

* Intervention by Trudy Post Sprunk, LMFT-S, LPC-S, RPT-S™, PTI-S. Adapted from "Toss the Ball," by T. Post Sprunk, in L. Lowenstein (Ed.), *Creative Family Therapy Techniques: Play, Art, and Expressive Activities to Engage Children in Family Sessions* (2010), Champion Press.

4. The third round of the game involves what is said when one catches the ball. The person who catches the ball must say something they would like to change about themselves and what prevents their ability to make that change. Allow time for the family to process and develop strategies for change. Possible discussion questions include:

    - List two things that would serve as aids to making the change that you would like to make.

    - On a scale of 1 to 10, how important is this change to you? To others in your family?

    - In what ways would your family life be improved after these changes were made?

5. In the final round, when one person tosses the ball to another, the recipient shares an idea about what they could do to improve their family life. After each person has had a turn, encourage the family to consider all the suggestions and decide whether and how these suggestions can be incorporated into their family life.

TOTEM OF APPRECIATION

Introduction

This activity is an adapted version of the game Totem. The goal is for family members to recognize, appreciate, and reinforce the positive qualities in one another, fostering a stronger emotional connection and family attachment.

Goals

- Help family members recognize, appreciate, and reinforce the positive qualities in one another
- Improve positive interaction within the family

Materials

- Totem card game

Instructions

1. The Totem game comes with animal cards (representing strengths or personality traits) and quality cards (representing positive adjectives). The game is played as usual, with an added component in which each family member says to the dealer something that they appreciate about them (e.g., "I appreciate when you help me with my homework," "I appreciate when you brighten my day with your smile").

2. After building the totem, the family discusses the cards chosen and the statements of appreciation. The family member in the totem seat listens and reflects on the feedback.

3. Over time, as each family member's totem is built, a family totem tower is created, representing the collective strengths and positive connections shared among them. This visual representation grows with each player's round.

4. The game ends when everyone has had a turn in the totem seat, and the family reflects on the experience. Prompt them to discuss how recognizing each other's strengths has deepened their attachment and appreciation for one another.

5. Ask process questions such as:
   - How did it feel to hear these things about yourself?
   - How does positive feedback impact the relationships within your family?
   - How can you consistently give positive feedback to one another?

UPSIDE-DOWN TOWER OF POSITIVES*

Introduction

In this collaborative exercise, family members use Jenga blocks to build a unique tower while identifying positive characteristics they appreciate about each other, shared memories, and activities they enjoy together. The goal is to enhance positive self-perception and foster positive family interactions through communication and appreciation.

Goals

- Increase positive feelings about self
- Increase positive interaction among family members

Materials

- Jenga game

Instructions

1. Scatter all the blocks on the table. Encourage the family members to start thinking of positive characteristics they appreciate about each other, activities they enjoy doing together, what makes them special, and memories they have together.

2. Have the family members take turns adding one block at a time to build a tower. With each block added, that player shares aloud something positive about one of their family members or about their family as a whole. The participants get to determine what they would like the tower to look like, as it does not need to look like the typical Jenga tower.

3. Ask process questions such as:
   - How did it feel to hear positive things about yourself from your family members?
   - How do you think focusing on positive traits can help your family?
   - What did you notice about the way you worked together to build the tower?

---

* Intervention by Kelly Pullen, MA, LPC-S, RPT™

WHAT WOULD THEY SAY?*

AGES: 8+   **MODALITY:** FAMILY

Introduction

This fun and interactive game aims to assess family relationships, encourage open communication, and explore underlying emotions within the family dynamic. Through a combination of a quick-paced game like Jenga or KerPlunk and a series of engaging questions, family members will have the chance to guess each other's responses, fostering greater understanding and family cohesion in a playful, supportive environment.

Goals

- Assess family relationships and dynamics
- Increase open communication among family members
- Encourage participants to share feelings that underlie conflict within the family
- Increase family cohesion

Materials

- Question cards (provided)
- Colored cardstock
- Scissors
- Jenga or KerPlunk (or another fast-paced game where players get many turns)
- Paper and writing utensils

Advance Preparation

- Copy the question cards onto colored cardstock and cut them out. Do not shuffle the cards—order them deliberately so that participants will draw neutral questions first, questions that require greater emotional risk later, and questions that elicit happy feelings last, to end the game on a positive note. The family members should get an equal number of turns as each other during the game, so select an appropriate number of cards. Omit or modify questions as needed to suit the family members and their treatment goals.

Instructions

1. Give each family member a sheet of paper and a writing utensil.

2. Decide which family member will go first. If this is difficult for the family to decide, have them roll a die or use some other chance method to decide who will go first. The turns then go clockwise.

---

* Intervention by Greg Lubimiv, MSW, CPT-S. Adapted from "What Would They Say?" by G. Lubimiv, in L. Lowenstein (Ed.), *Creative Family Therapy Techniques: Play, Art, and Expressive Activities to Engage Children in Family Sessions* (2010), Champion Press.

3. Play Jenga or KerPlunk as normal. When a turn is over because the tower or marbles have fallen, that player picks the top card from the question card pile, reads the prompt aloud, and secretly writes their answer on the card. The other family members write down on their sheet of paper what they think that player's answer is.

4. The responses are then read aloud. Each correct answer scores one point. Emphasize that an important rule of the game is for everyone to accept whatever answer a family member may give, even—especially—when they disagree. If a family member becomes upset with another person's answer, remind them of the rule and offer support, or ask another family member to provide some support.

5. As the content of the cards asks the players to provide more emotional or vulnerable responses, explore them with the family. For example, if a player shares, "When I get mad, you can tell because I... shout," ask, "Who else shouts in your family?"

6. The game continues until each family member has had their predetermined number of turns (the cards you preselected have all been used). At the end of the game, the person with the most points wins.

7. Optional: To make the game noncompetitive, challenge the family to reach a certain score together. For example, if there are 20 questions and four family members, the highest score is 60 (because one person does not guess each round, as they completed the sentence). Choose a score that the family could reasonably achieve. In our example, you might decide a combined score of 30 means the family wins.

8. Ask process questions such as:
   - What was the most interesting or surprising response?
   - What did this game reveal about who you know best/least in your family?
   - What did you like best about this game?

WHAT WOULD THEY SAY? QUESTION CARDS

?? My favorite color is . . .	**??** My favorite food is . . .	**??** My favorite fruit is . . .	**??** A food I hate is . . .
?? My favorite ice cream flavor is . . .	**??** My favorite animal is . . .	**??** My favorite TV show is . . .	**??** My favorite thing to do is . . .
?? If choosing between chocolate and potato chips, I would choose . . .	**??** Between going for a walk and watching a good movie, I would choose . . .	**??** Between a bath and a shower, I prefer . . .	**??** The person in my family who laughs the most is . . .
?? My favorite season is . . .	**??** The person in my family who helps others the most is . . .	**??** My favorite room in the house is . . .	**??** Something our family needs more of is . . .
?? My favorite holiday is . . .	**??** My favorite breakfast food is . . .	**??** I feel most loved by my family when they . . .	**??** My favorite thing to do all together as a family is . . .

CHAPTER 9

Facilitating a Positive Termination

The termination phase in therapy is a crucial part of the therapeutic process, marking the closure of the client-therapist relationship. It serves as a time to consolidate the progress the client has made and ensure they feel empowered to continue using the skills they've developed. To ensure a successful termination, the therapist must attend to several key areas. Reviewing progress and celebrating the client's successes is essential, as it allows the therapist and client to reflect on the journey, highlighting the growth experienced and emphasizing changes in how the client manages their thoughts, emotions, and behaviors. Reinforcing the tools and strategies the client has acquired during therapy is equally important, with games being a useful way to review skills learned throughout the sessions. Another key focus of termination is addressing future challenges the client may face. This discussion helps the client feel prepared to apply the skills they've learned in real-life situations after therapy ends.

Incorporating games during the termination phase of therapy can provide a meaningful, engaging, and memorable closure for clients. Using games to frame the goodbye in a positive, celebratory manner makes the process less about loss and more about the recognition of growth. Games also offer a comfortable platform for clients to process and express emotions about the end of therapy, allowing them to reminisce while recognizing their progress. They serve as a way to reinforce therapeutic lessons by revisiting key concepts and skills, boosting the client's confidence in their ability to apply what they have learned. Ending therapy with a positive, playful activity creates lasting memories of the therapeutic process, making it more likely that clients will have positive attitudes toward seeking help in the future if needed.

BALLOON BASH

Introduction

This activity helps children review and evaluate their experiences in therapy. The balloon is symbolic of the celebratory nature of this termination activity and is given to the client at the end as a parting gift.

Goals

- Review and consolidate skills learned in therapy
- Experience a positive ending from therapy

Materials

- *Balloon Bash Prompts* (provided)
- Two balloons
- Timer

Advance Preparation

- Blow up two balloons and knot them. (Only one balloon is needed for the game, but it is recommended to have an extra balloon on hand in case one pops during the activity.)
- Review the provided prompts and modify them so they are geared to the client's age and issues addressed in therapy.

Instructions

1. Explain: "You have worked hard in therapy and you have learned so much! This game is called Balloon Bash. It will help you talk about some of the things you did in therapy. To play, throw the balloon up in the air and try to keep it in the air for 30 seconds without it touching the ground. Then I will ask you a question."

2. After 30 seconds (or after the balloon touches the ground), ask the client a question from your list. Repeat until all the questions have been answered.

3. The client can take the balloon home as a celebration of all their hard work in therapy.

BALLOON BASH PROMPTS

General

- You learned to express your feelings. Name three feelings that children coping with [*presenting issue*] may have.

- Children have different feelings about ending sessions. Some children feel happy about ending, some feel upset, and some feel both. How do you feel about ending sessions?

- What advice would you give to a child who is experiencing [*presenting problem*]?

- We did many activities together in therapy. Which activity did you like best?

- What would you tell someone who is just starting therapy?

- You learned about [*presenting problem*]. What are some of the things you learned?

- Tell about something that you did in therapy that helped you.

Divorce

- You learned ways to handle the stress of going back and forth between two homes. Say something you can do to cope with going back and forth between two homes.

- You learned that even though your parents are divorced, you are still a family, and you can have fun times with Mom and fun times with Dad. Tell about a fun time with Mom, then tell about a fun time with Dad.

- You learned ways to handle when your parents argue. Practice saying to yourself, "Even when my parents argue, they still love me no matter what!"

Anxiety

- You learned that when you are scared or worried, your body feels different. What is one thing that happens in your body when you feel scared or worried?

- You learned ways to relax your body. Pretend you are feeling scared or worried and show what you can do to relax your body.

- You learned that thinking calm, helpful thoughts makes you feel better. Which of these is a calm, helpful thought that can help you feel better: "This is too scary; I can't do this" or "I have proven that I can do hard things. I can handle this."

- You learned to face your fear. What is something that used to make you feel really worried or scared that you are able to do now without feeling so worried or scared?

Grief

- You learned many ways to help yourself through tough times. What are some ways you can help yourself feel better when you are upset in the future?

- What advice would you give to a child who is grieving?

THE FAMILY BOWL*

AGES: 8+   **MODALITY:** FAMILY

Introduction

This game can be played in one of the last sessions as part of the termination process to help family members articulate and visually represent the progress they have made in therapy. It serves as a meaningful way to reflect on therapeutic gains and reinforce positive changes within the family.

Goals

- Verbally articulate progress made in therapy
- Provide a visual reminder of therapeutic gains

Materials

- Large bowl filled with pinto beans or another type of dry bean
- Smaller bowls and spoons
- Timer (optional for added challenge)

Instructions

1. Place the full bowl of pinto beans in the middle of the table. (Keep a small amount of beans hidden in reserve for the optional bonus round later.) Provide each player with a smaller bowl and a spoon.

2. **Round 1—Taking from the Family Bowl:** Each player takes turns scooping beans from the large bowl into their smaller bowl. While doing so, they share something they felt was lacking or challenging in the family when they first started therapy. Continue until the large bowl is empty.

3. **Round 2—Refilling the Family Bowl:** Each player takes turns scooping beans from their small bowl back into the large family bowl while sharing a specific positive change or action they have contributed to the family (e.g., talking respectfully, using appropriate techniques to self-calm when angry, following house rules, responding to first requests, using an inside voice, saying please and thank you more often, helping with chores, cleaning up after themselves). The family earns one point each time someone shares a positive change or action they have contributed to the family. Continue until the large bowl is full.

4. **(Optional) Bonus Round—The Challenge of Reflection:** Present the extra beans that you had kept hidden and divide them equally among the family members' small bowls. Set a timer for two minutes. Each player must quickly think of another specific way they have contributed positively and share it while adding their bonus beans to the family bowl. Each additional specific action shared within the time limit earns the family an extra point.

---

* Intervention by Norma Leben, LCSW-S, ACSW, RPT-S™ (retired)

5. **Final Round—Feelings Reflection:** Ask each player to share how they feel seeing the bowl refilled again. Each player earns a point for sharing a feeling word and another point if they can explain why they feel that way.

6. Calculate the total points the family earned and congratulate them on their victory. (They necessarily win by refilling their family bowl.) Emphasize how hard they have worked and how much progress they have made in therapy.

7. Ask process questions such as:

   - How did it feel to share something positive you have done for your family?
   - Which actions do you think were the most helpful to the family? Why?
   - How can we keep the "family bowl" full of good things after our sessions are over?
   - What did you learn about your family through this activity?

LAST SESSION FAMILY CARD GAME*

AGES: 7+   **MODALITY:** FAMILY

Introduction

This card game is designed to provide families with a meaningful and positive closure to their therapy experience. Through engaging questions, the game helps family members reflect on their therapeutic progress, acknowledge individual and collective growth, and express their feelings about ending therapy.

Goals

- Review and validate therapeutic gains
- Verbally identify and discuss feelings about ending therapy
- Provide a positive termination experience

Materials

- Question cards (provided)
- Cardstock or index cards
- Scissors
- Standard 52-card deck
- Cookies or other reward items

Advance Preparation

- Photocopy the questions onto cardstock and cut them into cards (or copy the questions onto index cards).

Instructions

1. Introduce the game by saying, "We are going to play a game that will help you talk about your experiences in therapy, your accomplishments in therapy, and your feelings about ending therapy." If the family played the First Session Family Card Game (page 4) at the beginning of their therapy, reference that experience and note that this time the game is about ending therapy.

2. Explain the rules: "Take turns picking the top card from the deck of cards. If you get a card with an even number, pick a question card and answer the question. If you get a card with an odd number, pick a question card and ask someone in your family to answer the question. If you do not feel you can answer the question, you can ask your family for help. If you pick an ace, ask someone in your family for a hug, fist bump, or high five. If you pick a jack, do 10 jumping jacks. If you pick a queen or king, you get a cookie."

---

* Adapted from "Last Session Family Card Game," by L. Lowenstein, in L. Lowenstein (Ed.), *Creative Family Therapy Techniques: Play, Art, and Expressive Activities to Engage Children in Family Sessions* (2010), Champion Press.

3. Observe the gameplay, highlighting individual and family changes during the course of therapy and reinforcing strengths.

4. At the end of the game, give everyone a cookie.

5. Ask process questions such as:

   - What do you think was the purpose of this game?

   - Whose answers were most like how you feel?

   - What positive changes did you notice in how your family interacted during this game, compared to how you interacted at the beginning of therapy?

LAST SESSION FAMILY CARD GAME: QUESTION CARDS

?? What is a positive change you have made during your time in therapy?	**??** What is a positive change someone in your family has made during your time in therapy?	**??** Change seats with the person who you think worked the hardest in therapy.
?? Tell about a skill you learned in therapy that you can use to deal with problems that arise in the future.	**??** Tell about something you have learned about someone in your family during your time in therapy.	**??** What helped you the most during your time in therapy?
?? Name someone who can help you when you have a problem or a worry.	**??** Fill in the blank: Something our family needs to continue to work on is...	**??** What is your family able to do better now?
?? What was your favorite activity that you did in therapy?	**??** Fill in the blank: My proudest moment in therapy was when I...	**??** How do you feel about ending therapy?
?? What advice would you give to another family who are experiencing a problem similar to the one that brought you to therapy?	**??** What's something that a family member did in therapy that you appreciated?	**??** Families often teach therapists valuable lessons. Ask your therapist to tell something your family has taught them.

MINUTE TO WIN IT

Introduction

This termination game helps children practice and reinforce skills learned in therapy, particularly in emotional regulation and self-esteem. By completing quick, engaging tasks within a minute, children can review their progress in a rewarding way, ensuring a positive ending to their therapeutic journey.

Goals

- Review and consolidate skills learned in therapy
- Experience a positive termination from therapy

Materials

- Paper
- Pen
- Trash can
- Balloon
- Timer
- Small, inexpensive prizes

Advance Preparation

- Review the examples of tasks included in the instructions and adapt them so they are appropriate to your client's age and therapeutic goals.

Instructions

1. Explain: "Today we're going to do a fun activity to help you practice some of the things you have learned in therapy. I will ask you to complete a series of tasks. If you complete a task in under one minute, you get a point. At the end, you will trade in your points for prizes!"

2. Prompt the client to perform tasks and time them to see if they can complete each task in one minute or less. Here are some examples of tasks:

   - Write down five emotions.
   - Write down three healthy coping strategies you can use if you feel [*presenting issue*].
   - Pretend you are feeling [*presenting issue*]. Demonstrate deep breathing that might help you settle.
   - Bonus point: Crumple a piece of paper to form a ball. Stand behind the designated line. Throw the crumpled paper into the trash can.
   - Draw a picture of yourself using a healthy coping strategy to manage [*presenting issue*].
   - Name three good things about yourself.
   - Write down three things you learned in therapy.
   - Write down three things you feel proud of.
   - Bonus point: Blow up a balloon and knot it. Keep it in the air without it touching the ground.

3. At the end, trade in the client's points for prizes: 1–8 points = 1 prize, 9 or more points = 2 prizes.

4. Ask process questions such as:

   - What was it like to practice the skills you learned in therapy?

   - What are you most proud of from our time together?

   - What advice would you give someone who's just starting therapy?

NATURE SHAPES SCAVENGER HUNT*

AGES: 5+   **MODALITY:** GROUP, FAMILY

Introduction

This activity helps clients reflect on their journey, celebrate their growth, and consolidate the skills they've learned. Through finding shapes in nature and using them as discussion prompts, participants can share their memories, express gratitude, and look forward to the future, fostering a meaningful closure to their therapy.

Goals

- Review the therapeutic journey
- Focus on the positive impact of the therapy

Materials

- Access to an outdoor space where nature items can be found
- Paper and coloring utensils

Instructions

1. Explain: "This game will help you to share about your experiences in therapy and working together. Each of you will have an opportunity to share using shapes we find in nature. To start, you will go on a scavenger hunt to find as many different shapes in nature as you can. If the item is small and okay for you to take, like a fallen leaf, please bring it back to the group circle. If the item is larger or not okay to take, like a tree, please write down or draw what the item is. You can also group items together to create shapes—for example, you could put small rocks on the ground in the shape of a heart."

2. Set an appropriate time limit for the clients to find the nature items. Once everyone has returned from the scavenger hunt, have them sit a circle with the nature items in the middle.

3. Have the participants take turns selecting a nature item, and prompt them to share based on the item's shape:
   - **Heart:** Tell about someone who supported you during therapy.
   - **Circle:** Who is in your circle of care—who are your supports?
   - **Triangle:** When was a time you took meaningful action or made a positive change during therapy?
   - **Square:** Name something that stood out to you during therapy that you want to remember or reflect on more.
   - **Rectangle:** When was a time during therapy when you helped someone else in the group/family?
   - **Tree:** Tell about how you have grown during your time in therapy.

---

* Intervention by Lynette Nikkel MSW, RSW

- **Flower:** Tell about how someone else in the group/family has blossomed.
- **Star:** Share a hope you have for the future.

4. Ask process questions such as:

- What was the most surprising or interesting shape in nature that you found, and why?
- How did sharing about your experiences using the nature shapes help you reflect on your therapy journey?
- Which shape or item was the easiest for you to talk about, and which was the most challenging? Why?

THERAPY TREASURE HUNT*

Introduction

This game is designed to facilitate a positive termination of mental health therapy by reflecting on the client's progress, celebrating their achievements, and encouraging them to express their feelings about the therapeutic journey.

Goals

- Articulate progress made in therapy
- Discuss the client's experiences and reflect on their time in therapy
- Experience a positive ending to the therapeutic relationship

Materials

- Small cardboard treasure chest (or create one using a box)
- Index cards or cardstock
- Coloring utensils
- Decorative craft supplies (e.g., gem stickers, glitter glue)

Advance Preparation

- Write various reflection prompts on index cards or small pieces of cardstock. Examples include:
  - A skill I learned in therapy that I find helpful is . . .
  - My favorite memory from therapy is . . .
  - Something I will continue to work on is . . .
  - A way I have grown is . . .
  - Something I want to thank my therapist for is . . .
  - I'm proud of myself for...
- Hide the cards in various places around the room or office. Be sure to note where each card is hidden so they can all be found.

Instructions

1. Explain to the client that this game is a fun way to celebrate their progress and reflect on how they have grown in therapy. Let them know they will go on a treasure hunt to find and share their achievements and memories.

2. Have the client search for the reflection prompt cards around the room. As each card is found, discuss the prompt and have the client draw or write their response on the card. Invite the client to decorate the cards if desired. Place the completed cards in the treasure chest.

---

* Intervention by Andrea Dorn, MSW, LISW-CP

3. Continue until all prompts have been found and answered or a set amount of time has passed (e.g., 10–15 minutes).

4. Once the treasure chest is full, the child can decorate the outside of the chest with additional stickers and decorations.

5. Celebrate the child's progress by acknowledging their hard work and growth. Present the decorated treasure chest to the client as a keepsake to remember their therapy journey and the important tools they learned.

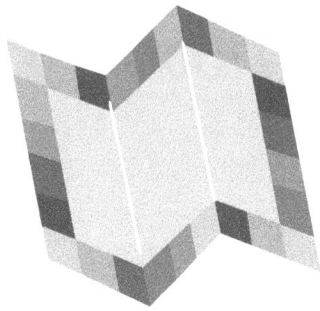

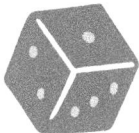

Appendix

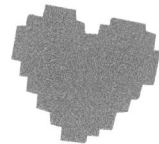

GET TO KNOW YOU QUESTIONS

- What do you like to do in your free time?

- What's one of your favorite TV shows?

- What's one of your favorite snack foods?

- Who is one of your favorite celebrities?

- If you could travel to anywhere in the world, where would you go?

- What is something you wish you had more of?

- If you could make one rule for your family, what would it be?

- If you had three wishes, what would you wish for?

- If you could meet anyone, who would you choose?

- Where is your favorite place?

- What's your favorite holiday and why?

- What's one of the best gifts you ever received?

- What's something that really annoys you?

- What was one moment in your life when you felt really proud?

- What is one of your favorite things to do?

- When is your birthday?

- If you could have anything for dessert, what would it be?

- What is one of your favorite toys?

- If you could choose any name, what would it be?

- What is one of your favorite dinners?

- If you could be any animal, what would it be?

- If you could put any two toppings on an ice cream sundae, what would they be?

- If you could choose any age to be, what would you choose?

- What is one of your favorite sports?

- What is one of your favorite fruits?

- If you could have any superpower, what would it be?

- What is one of your favorite candies?

- What's one of your favorite things to do?

- What's one of your favorite colors?

- What's one of your favorite animals?

- What's one of your favorite movies?

- If you could travel anywhere, where would you go?

- If you could have any superpower, what would you choose and why?

- If you could have dinner with someone famous, who would you choose?

- What's one of your favorite foods?

- What's something you feel thankful for?

- What's one of the most fun things you ever did?

FEELINGS WORDS

Accepted	Excited	Pleased
Adventurous	Exhausted	Proud
Afraid	Focused	Quiet
Angry	Friendly	Regretful
Annoyed	Frustrated	Relaxed
Ashamed	Gentle	Relieved
Awkward	Grateful	Resentful
Bored	Grumpy	Restless
Brave	Guilty	Rushed
Calm	Happy	Sad
Cautious	Hesitant	Safe
Challenged	Hopeful	Satisfied
Cheerful	Hurt	Scared
Comfortable	Ignored	Self-conscious
Confident	Impatient	Shy
Conflicted	Inspired	Silly
Confused	Irritated	Startled
Content	Jealous	Stressed
Creative	Joyful	Strong
Curious	Kind	Surprised
Daydreamy	Lonely	Suspicious
Delighted	Loved	Tense
Determined	Loving	Thankful
Disappointed	Mad	Thoughtful
Disgusted	Nervous	Tired
Disheartened	Optimistic	Trusting
Distracted	Overwhelmed	Uncertain
Embarrassed	Panicked	Wistful
Encouraged	Peaceful	Worried
Energetic	Playful	

TRAUMA BODY REACTIONS

Aching
Burning
Butterflies
Clamminess
Clenching
Cold
Crying
Discomfort
Dizziness
Dryness
Emptiness
Fainting
Faster breathing
Faster heartbeat
Feeling "not right"
Feeling dirty
Feeling disconnected
Feeling faint
Feeling frozen
Feeling far away
Feeling unreal
Feeling out of control
Fidgeting
Flinching
Flushing
Fluttering
Going to the bathroom less
Going to the bathroom more
Goosebumps
Headache
Heaviness
Hot
Jitters

Jumping
Less hungry than usual
Lightness
More hungry than usual
Nausea
Nightmares
Numbness
Pain
Pounding
Scary memories
Scary thoughts
Shaking
Skin crawling
Soreness
Spinning
Stiffness
Stomachache
Sweating
Tearing up
Tense muscles
Throwing up
Tightness
Tingling
Tiredness
Trouble breathing
Trouble concentrating
Trouble falling asleep
Trouble speaking
Trouble staying asleep
Trouble swallowing
Vision changes
Voice shaking
Weakness

ANGER SCENARIOS

- Someone took your favorite toy without asking.

- You were left out of a game at recess.

- Your sibling got a bigger slice of cake.

- You spilled juice on your new shirt.

- You lost a game with your friends.

- You lost a game you really wanted to win.

- Your friend said something mean to you.

- You were blamed for something you didn't do.

- You have to go to bed earlier than usual.

- Your sibling broke your favorite toy.

- You were told you can't have a pet.

- Someone pushed in front of you in line.

- You planned to have cereal for breakfast but there's none left.

- Your friend was supposed to come over but canceled.

- You're put in a group for a class art project with kids you don't like.

- Your friend wants to play outside but you would rather play inside.

- You were all set to go on a picnic outside, but it suddenly starts to rain.

- You were about to play with your favorite toy, but it suddenly breaks.

- The shoe store ran out of your size in the shoes you really wanted.

- You're playing a computer game and suddenly the power goes off.

- You're at soccer practice and you realize you forgot your soccer shoes.

- Your sibling gets to stay up later than you.

- You are sitting with your friend at school at lunch time and you notice that they got a better snack than you.

- You have a cold, so you have to stay home while everyone else in your family gets to go to the carnival.

- You're playing a board game with your friend and they keep winning.

- Your team keeps losing.

- You get into a fight with someone in your class at school, and you get into trouble but your classmate doesn't.

- Your sibling got a new pair of shoes but you didn't.

- Your sibling gets to pick the show/movie to watch.

- Your friend got a video game that you really want.

- Someone else got the part that you wanted in the school play.

- You have to go home and take a bath instead of staying outside to play with your friends.

- You keep raising your hand in class but your teacher keeps picking other kids.

- Your sibling gets to sit beside your parent.

COPING SKILLS

BREATHING EXERCISES

- **Bee Breathing:** Take a deep breath in through your nose, then breathe out through your mouth while buzzing like a bee.

- **Birthday Candle Breathing:** Take a deep breath in through your nose like you're smelling your birthday cake . . . then blow out the candles!

- **Cookie Breathing:** Put your hand over your belly button and feel your tummy moving with this exercise. Breathe in through your nose for four seconds, like you're smelling some delicious cookies that just came out of the oven! They smell great, but they're too hot—so blow on the cookies to cool them down by breathing out through your mouth for four seconds.

- **Figure Eight Breathing:** Slowly breathe and draw a figure eight like this: Start at the center. Trace one loop as you breathe in for 1, 2, 3, 4 until you reach the center, then breathe out for 1, 2, 3, 4 along the loop to finish the figure eight.

- **Finger Breathing:** Slowly move your right index finger up one side and down the other side of each of your five fingers on your left hand. As you move your index finger up, breathe in through your nose. As you move your index finger down, breathe out through your mouth.

- **Three Breaths:** Take three slow, deep breaths in through your nose and out through your mouth.

GROUNDING AND MOVEMENT

- **Bubble Bath:** Take a peaceful bubble bath (or imagine you are taking one). What scents and sensations do you notice?

- **Cold Water:** Drink some cool water, or splash it on your face or neck.

- **Dance:** Move your body in any way that feels good—it can be silly if you want!

- **Drumming:** Play a soothing rhythm on a drum or with your hands.

- **Eat Something Crunchy:** Mindfully munch on a crunchy snack, like carrots or almonds.

- **Essential Oil:** Breathe in the scent of a calming essential oil.

- **Feel Your Heartbeat:** Place your hand over your heart and notice how it beats as you breathe slowly in and out.

- **Get Moving:** Do physical activity like running, jumping jacks, or stretching.

- **Rocking:** Gently rock your body back and forth, or swing on a swing.

- **Snapshot Body Scan:** Imagine you are taking a picture of each part of your body, starting with your head and going down to your toes. What do you feel in each part?

- **Soothing Sensations:** Pick a small item—like beads, a stress ball, or a smooth stone—and notice how it feels in your hands.

- **Stretching/Yoga:** Practice some stretches or yoga poses that you have learned and notice how your body feels.

- **Walking:** Take a walk (outside, if you can). What do you sense within and around you?

- **Wash It Off:** Take a soothing shower or bath.

PROGRESSIVE MUSCLE RELAXATION

- **Lemon Squeeze:** Imagine you're holding a lemon and squeezing it to make lemonade. Squeeze the juice out, then relax your hands.

- **Robot/Ragdoll:** Tighten your body like a stiff robot, then make your body go floppy like a ragdoll.

- **Spaghetti:** Stand up straight and stiff, tightening your body like uncooked spaghetti. Hold it for three seconds. Then go limp and wiggle your muscles like cooked spaghetti. Do this three times.

BILATERAL STIMULATION

- **Butterfly Hug:** Cross your arms over your chest and gently tap your fingertips against your collarbone, alternating left and right.

- **Scribble:** On a piece of paper, scribble a long, smooth zigzag from left, to right, to left, to right . . .

MINDFULNESS AND MEDITATION

- **Calm Place:** Create a detailed place in your imagination where you can go when you need to feel calm.

- **Count to 10:** Count slowly from 1 to 10 to calm your mind and body.

- **Glitter Jar:** Gently shake a glitter jar or snow globe and watch the glitter swirl.

- **Rainbow Noticing:** Look around and find something that corresponds with each color of a rainbow.

- **Three Things:** Identify three things you see around you to distract yourself from the upsetting feelings.

EXPRESSING FEELINGS

- **Draw Your Feelings:** Draw a picture to express your feelings.

- **Write It Down:** Write down what you are feeling in a journal.

GETTING SUPPORT

- **Ask for Support:** Ask an adult for help to understand and deal with the situation.

- **Share with an Adult:** Find an adult you trust and tell them what's bothering you.

- **Talk:** Talk to someone you trust about how you're feeling.

POSITIVE THOUGHTS

- **Gratitude:** Think of at least three good things in your life. These can be people, places, objects, times—anything that you feel thankful for.

- **Positive Self-Talk:** Say something helpful to yourself, like "I can handle this," "I can take things one step at a time," "Win some, lose some," or "I don't like what happened, but I choose to stay calm."

- **Proud Moment:** Think of a moment in your life when you felt proud.

- **Think Calm Thoughts:** You can use words (like "I breathe in peace and I breathe out worry"), picture something that helps you feel calm, or just remember what it feels like to be calm.

ENJOYABLE ACTIVITIES

- **Go Outside:** Sit or take a walk outside and notice the natural world around you.

- **Laugh:** Watch a funny video or think of something that makes you laugh.

- **Listen to Music:** Play your favorite songs and notice how your body feels.

- **Play:** Enjoy your favorite toys or games.

- **Read:** Find a cozy spot and read a book or article.

Acknowledgments

Creating this book on game therapy has been an inspiring and rewarding journey, and I am deeply grateful to the many individuals and teams who have made it possible.

First and foremost, my heartfelt thanks go to Kate Sample and the entire team at PESI for their exceptional work in bringing this book to life. Your meticulous editing, innovative design, and dedication to excellence have transformed this manuscript into a resource I am proud to share. Your professionalism and creativity have been invaluable throughout this process.

I would also like to express my gratitude to my colleagues who have contributed their creative therapeutic games. Your willingness to share your ideas and expertise has enriched this book immeasurably.

To my clients, thank you for being the ultimate source of inspiration. Your courage, resilience, and openness motivate me to continue designing therapeutic games that not only engage but also teach and heal. Your stories and progress remind me of the profound impact that creativity and play can have on the journey to well-being.

To my readers, thank you for your commitment to making a difference in the lives of others through the power of play. May this book engage your clients in game play and help them grow, heal, and make meaningful, lasting change.

Lastly, I extend my deepest gratitude to my friends and family, whose unwavering support has been a cornerstone of this journey. A special thanks to my daughter, Jaime, and my husband, Steven, for their love and encouragement.

With deepest gratitude,

Liana

List of Contributors

Rachel Altvater, PsyD, RPT-S™

Brian L. Bethel, LPCC-S, LCDC III, RPT-S™

Angela Cavett, PhD

Laura Chackes, PsyD

Katy Delagardelle, LISW

Andrea Dorn, MSW, LISW-CP

Ivey Drawdy, MS, LPC

Pam Dyson, MA, LPC, RPT-S™

Sheri Eggleton, Hons. RP, CTIC

Elizabeth Ernest, LMFT, LCSW

Kathy Eugster, MA, RCC, CPT-S

Ellie Finch, MA, MBACP (Accred.)

Paris Goodyear-Brown, LCSW, RPT-S™

Robert Jason Grant EdD, LPC, RPT-S™

Batsheva Hartstein, LCSW-C, RPT-S™

Dina Ismailova, LCPC

Jamie Lynn Langley, LCSW, RPT-S™

Norma Leben, LCSW-S, ACSW, RPT-S™ (retired)

Greg Lubimiv, MSW, CPT-S

Ann Meehan, MS, LPCC, RPT-S™, EMDRIA consultant

Tasha Milligan, MA, LPC, RPT™

Lauren Mosback, LPC, NCC

Katie Musa, PhD, IMFT-S, LPCC-S, RPT™

Lynette Nikkel, MSW, RSW

Sueann Kenney-Noziska, MSW, LCSW, RPT-S™

Niki Picogna, PsyD, LCPC, LPC, LMHC, RPT-S™

Trudy Post Sprunk, LMFT-S, LPC-S, RPT-S™, PTI-S

Kelly Pullen, MA, LPC-S, RPT™

Lisa Remey, MEd, LPC-S, NCC, RPT-S™

Scott Riviere, MS, LPC, LMFT, RPT-S™

Arlen Sarabia, PhD

Tracy Turner-Bumberry, LPC, RPT-S™, CAS

Tammi Van Hollander, LCSW, RPT-S™

Janet Vessels, PhD, LPCC-S, RPT-S™

Erika Walker, LSCSW, LCSW, LICSW, RPT-S™

Holly Willard, LCSW, RPT-S™

Lynn Louise Wonders, LPC, RPT-S™, CPCS, DCC

Gary G. F. Yorke, PhD

Fiona Zandt, D.Psych, RPT™

About the Author

Liana Lowenstein, MSW, RSW, CPT-S, is a registered social worker, certified TF-CBT therapist, and certified play therapist-supervisor who has been working with children and their families in Toronto since 1988. She provides clinical consultation to mental health practitioners and presents trainings across North America and abroad. She is the founder of Champion Press Publishing Company and has authored numerous publications, which are used by mental health professionals all over the world. She is a recipient of the Monica Herbert Award for outstanding contributions to play therapy in Canada.